While Still There Is Light

While Still There Is Light

Writings from a Minister Facing Death

Nancy Shaffer

Edited by Mary McKinnon Ganz

Skinner House Books
Boston

www.skinnerhouse.org

Printed in the United States

Cover and text design by Suzanne Morgan
Front cover photo by Julie Voelck. Used with permission

print ISBN: 978-1-55896-700-7
eBook ISBN: 978-1-55896-701-4

6 5 4 3 2 1
15 14 13

Library of Congress Cataloging-in-Publication Data
Shaffer, Nancy.
  While still there is light : writings from a minister facing death / Nancy Shaffer;
Mary Ganz, editor.
     pages cm
  ISBN 978-1-55896-700-7 (pbk. : alk. paper)—ISBN 978-1-55896-701-4 (ebook)
1. Spirituality—Unitarian Universalist churches. 2. Death—Religious aspects—
Unitarian Universalist churches. I. Ganz, Mary. II. Title.
  BX9855.S53 2013
  289.1092—dc23
                                                                    2012042586

I tried to hold on to knowing
until I could waken.
I was clear:
the only question large enough
is how to give enough thanks for our lives.
That's the beginning:
large enough thanks.

—Nancy Shaffer

Contents

Preface

In the third week of June, 2011, I ducked out of a workshop happening at the Unitarian Universalist General Assembly in Charlotte, to call my friend Nancy, who had had surgery, less than two weeks previous, to remove a fist-sized tumor from the right frontal lobe of her brain. By then, Nancy had received the report of the pathologist, and we had not yet talked about it. In this conversation, we still didn't.

Instead, with great clarity and purpose, Nancy told me what she had figured out about her life in a new landscape. Three things matter, she told me. First, seek wholeness. What that meant for her would become clear in the seeking. Second, create and live in beauty; that was about writing, primarily. Three, pay attention to relationships: be present to people; allow people to be present to her.

In this way, Nancy said, she intended to live. Details of the pathology report—which I had dreaded to hear—faded against the vividness of the priorities Nancy had envisioned for herself. Her words sounded with bell-like clarity against the background buzz of the vast convention hall, where I was listening, six hundred miles away.

As the days unfolded, these priorities resolved themselves into a project to write her life. It would be a book that would share the day-to-day experiences, thoughts, and feelings of a poet, a minister, an individual in a fight for her life, a human being facing life-limiting illness. It would share the beauty, the terror, the reality of the experience. This would be a book for ministers, writers, doctors, technicians, nurses, spouses, adult children, anyone caring for someone with life-limiting illness, and especially for people experiencing such an illness. In short, anyone.

Nancy was just the person to do this. She was an accomplished poet whose collection *Instructions in Joy* (2002) had inspired me and countless colleagues and readers for a decade; a minister, whose clear-eyed compassion and courage vouchsafed her entry to the most tender and terrifying regions of the soul; a person who had faced demons in her own nearly 61 years of living, and learned much.

However, there might not be time to finish the book. This is where I would step in—carefully, tentatively, with only the lightest of touch, to assemble notes, journal entries and poems Nancy had written by the end of whatever time she had. It turned out to be one year—one vibrant, hugely productive, joyous year—living as a minister with her eyes wide open to the reality of her own finitude.

Nancy and I had shared poems and ministry over the years of our friendship, which spanned a dozen years. We brought to each other problems in our ministries; questions about relationships; and often, poems.

Over the course of the 11 months she wrote them, Nancy sent me about two thirds of the writings included here. The others I received from our colleague, Leslie Takahashi Morris, who—as Nancy began to struggle with saving documents on a computer—copied her hard drive and sent the writings to me in a Dropbox account.

I have edited these pieces with a light hand, trying to imagine what suggested changes Nancy would approve, if she and I were discussing them over phone or over email, as we did with so many shared writings over the years of our friendship. I have, in a few pieces, removed or blurred identification of the subject, in order to protect Nancy's privacy, or the privacy of others. I did this only after deep consideration.

Nancy wrote to hold a light for those who come after her; always the minister, this need to serve was strong in her heart. Stronger still was her need to give thanks. She wrote because she had to write, the way she had to breathe; writing was "air before air," writing was prayer; in it, she gave voice to the deep gratitude she felt for the incomprehensible gift of living—drawing one breath, and then another. It has been my joy and honor to participate in this work of thanksgiving. In it, my friend, Nancy Shaffer, lives; her light goes on.

How to Read This Book

This is a story told in fragments—recorded thoughts and questions, prayers, notes, and poems. The narrative emerges gradually, in soft focus, from these writings, which track the movement of Nancy's mind and heart during this challenging and beautiful year. I have arranged them chronologically as Nancy dated them. I think this matches her intention for this book, but— compromised as she was in the time-keeping, sequencing center of her brain—she felt confounded by the task, a frustration that surfaces repeatedly in her writing.

A few pieces did not include dates; in those cases I often had dates on the emails when I received them, or dates from her hard drive when she saved them, so I was able to place them in the chronology. Because these pieces are presented in the order written and not in the order of experience, the reader may notice a certain layering of detail—a journal entry about an experience comes back later as a poem, for example. Especially, the primary experiences and insights gained at the time of her surgery and diagnosis resurface throughout the year, as she continued to think about them and make meaning of them. This texture recalls Nancy's aesthetic in crafting worship.

Nancy wrote first thoughts longhand on a yellow pad, then entered pieces into the computer, often with line breaks indicating the beginning of the poems they would become as she refined them further. Included here are writings from all stages of her process—from journal logs to poetic skeletons to finished poems. Here, you will find some pieces that recall the beautiful, finished poems in *Instructions in Joy*, in which each is a small masterpiece of spiritual insight. Here, you will also find poems and journal entries that are raw, rough, more distant from revelation, reflecting the meaning that can be found in immediate experience. The writings shine Nancy's searching light on the depths of fear and knowledge that accompany us when we contemplate finitude. They also offer insight into the actual, day-to-day emotional reality of losing one's hair, deciding what to eat and how to care for a body, how a mind whose time-perception is compromised by illness manages to follow elaborate medication and fasting schedules, how the usual catastrophes of daily living—landlord troubles, tax deadlines, misunderstood instructions to delivery people—are magnified in the midst of major illness. All of it is here—life at once "nuts and sublime," as Nancy put it.

Here you will find a powerful spiritual voice, and unprocessed pain. You will see a *whole person*—one who finds meaning and beauty in a terrible truth, one who chuckles at life's ironies and human foibles, and also one who screams in rage.

I struggled with how much rage to leave in the book. I was pretty clear that Nancy intended to include most of what I came to think of as the "anger poems." Anger is a human response to pain and invasion, and Nancy had experienced plenty of both in her lifetime, so she had a particularly sensitive antenna for them. She gives us the benefit of this sensitivity when she instructs us how to write a card to a person who is ill, or invites us to think carefully before we say the first thing that pops into our minds. ("Listen up!" she tells us. "Just say hello"—without the added questions about what drugs a person may be taking that make her face rounder than you remembered.)

Some of the anger poems target her family. Few know the full history and context, but I do know this: When the cancer struck, Nancy was taking steps, slowly and deliberately, toward reconciling with her parents. Her need to put her entire attention on her own healing caused her to pull back from this process, which caused them pain, as will some of these writings. I also know this: In the last weeks of her life, Nancy asked to have her father and her mother with her, and they were there for her in very important ways.

Some of the anger pieces target other particular people—the thoughtless and sometimes well-intentioned folks she encountered on her path, and individuals with whom she had history. I have omitted some of these pieces. Others I kept in, but removed as much identifying information as possible, while remaining true to Nancy's writing. Some of these people may recognize themselves, and I sincerely regret any pain this causes. I invite anyone who feels stung to think of the anger not as personal but iconic. *Of course* someone facing an illness like this will rage. It was not Nancy's way to rage, like Job, at Creation; her anger found its particular objects, and only those who were in its path can judge whether there is any truth in it for them. As the editor, I am responsible for being truthful to Nancy, and this anger was a part of her. She was a whole person, and in her wholeness, she—like all of us—was broken.

One of the themes you will find in this book, and the driving force behind her writing, is *witness.* Nancy's life, before and after the tumor, was devoted to careful attentiveness to the worlds, inner and outer, and to finding exactly the right words to describe them. She saw the act of writing and the book that would result as a work of witness, one that would outlive her in ways that would bring healing to the world—her own experience, handed to us in truth and beauty, for a larger purpose.

Mary McKinnon Ganz
July 2012
Brewster, Massachusetts

Chronology

I offer here a brief outline of Nancy's year, not in an attempt to answer all the questions that might arise but as a simple map through terrain she traveled.

June   The tumor is discovered and removed; Nancy begins this book.

July   Beginning of a six-week course of radiation and chemotherapy. In this month Nancy looks with great courage at the diagnosis she has been given. There are also writings here that will be of interest especially to those who are traveling a similar path, those who are supporting a loved one along that path, and medical personnel who are supervising care.

August   Nancy feels the full effects of her treatment, and—still a minister to her core—begins to think of ways these rigors could be made easier for those who come after her.

September   As strength returns, so does memory, and she puts together pieces of what happened to her before the tumor was discovered.

October   Nancy appears once more for a worship service at the congregation she has served four years, to say goodbye.

November A colleague drives her across country to her former home in Davis, California, where she has decided to return to live and write. It is inconceivable that Nancy wrote nothing during this month, but the November writings are missing, both from her written files, and from her computer. A February poem tells of her discovery that "November" is missing. A file discovered in her home contained some raw writings; those that seemed complete or nearly so are included in this chapter.

December Nancy settles in to her condo in Davis, goes to church, and builds relationships with her new medical team.

January She joys in walking the Greenbelt, finding and rediscovering friendships, and especially writing.

February Nancy begins another course of treatment.

March It is harder to write now. Much of her energy, in this month and the next, is focused on food, and in getting her caregivers to understand what she needs. In this month and the next, she is hospitalized twice, spends a week in a rehab facility, and engages round-the-clock caregivers.

April This is the last month Nancy is writing. There are a few poems that are Nancy at her best, typed out one-handed over hours. Others are hasty and fragmentary.

May Nancy enters hospice care. Her parents take an apartment in Davis to assist with her care. When I visit toward the end of the month, she tells me, *I am learning so much.* I say, *I wish you could tell me what you are learning,* and she promises that she will find a way.

June   Nancy Morgan Shaffer dies on June 5, 2012. Her life is celebrated in memorial services held at the Unitarian Universalist Church of Davis, and the First Unitarian Universalist Congregation of Ann Arbor.

Introduction

Late in the evening of Sunday, June 5, 2011, after a precipitous April-May slide into exhaustion and something else I had no name for, I was admitted to the neurological intensive care unit of University of Michigan Hospital (UMHS) with an initial diagnosis of brain tumor. I was a little surprised to be admitted, but understood this meant something was really wrong—which I was relieved to know. A young doctor had said to me a couple of hours earlier—no preamble, no *maybe*s, no alternatives: "Lady, you've got a brain tumor. We've got to get it out." He was utterly calm, completely serious. I was grateful: some answers.

I wanted to go home—to get a few things (I knew exactly where they were; it would take me ten minutes) and to tell the cats what was up. UMHS wouldn't let me out. "No," I was told. "You must stay in ICU until we do surgery." Surgery needed to be very soon—like the next morning. The Catch-22 was that I had to have in place someone who could serve as local power of attorney and make decisions for my care on my behalf. Fine—except I am *not* local. I am still, after a total of eight years in the 1980s and four years more recently, not a *Mid*-Westerner but a *Westerner*—a bona fide, third-generation Californian. Some to whom I am close live on the East coast; most, on the West.

No local power of attorney, no surgery. So I set the wheels turning to put in place the taking of responsibility that would allow surgery. I made a list of colleagues who might serve, let other precious colleagues figure out the details. Drifted into sleep.

Surgery could not be scheduled until Thursday afternoon, June 9. By the next day, Friday, there was talk of sending me home on Saturday, if I had sufficient help (I live alone). Finally I went home on Tuesday, the 14th—nine days away in exchange for my life. A sweet and easy bargain.

I know myself and our world in large part through the reflective spiritual practice of writing. I woke up from surgery writing, made notes and began poems all during the days and through the nights, with little or no light. "Paper!" I would say to innocent nursing assistants and those who appeared to take my vitals. "Paper and another pen. Can you get that for me?" Orange juice did not matter at all.

I offer these poems and reflections as food for the journey— because each one of us will at some point come face to face with finiteness, and it is good to have friends who light the way. May this account be one such light.

—Nancy Shaffer

June

Who knew (well, I did)
that living
right at the center of life
would hold this much joy?

June 6

First Morning

Somewhere around five
on the morning after I've been hospitalized
I realize I'd better think through
not just where my possessions might go
but who may need to lead my memorial service.

The answer is immediate:
David and Mary. They get my theology.
We begin with that basis—
a baker's dozen years of knowing each other.
They would know immediately
how to shape this,
even though grieving.

David and I spoke once, walking,
after someone else's service.
The trees overhead were very tall,
dense with large leaves.

Lots of God, I'd said, *for mine.*
Good music.
A little about Jesus.
Not a lot about me.
Mostly it's thanks.

He had nodded, getting it perfectly.

They would weep—a lot—
but also would direct the cellists
where to sit
and when to play.
They would listen well.
It would all be okay.
Even glorious and worship.

David and Mary will know how to set all this up
and then get out of the way.

I am relieved that figuring out this much about the service is quick.
It isn't that I expect I will die, but I newly understand the need to
have people in place to take on what is needed.

Then I begin to think about to whom I should offer which of my
possessions. Most of this I decide quickly.

It's the cats and my writings I linger over. Both are essentially my
children.

June 11

First Words

Nic tells me the first thing I asked
after surgery was

Does God know it's over?

I don't remember asking that
but I *do* remember being aware
I'd been in the most intense spiritual experience
of my life—
and I didn't want to miss any of it.

I kept looking up
at a box of audio sorts of paraphernalia
near the ceiling of the room I was in,
thinking the blinking lights were related to
an interview that should be starting soon.
What I remember saying is something like

Somebody get me Krista Tippett!
I've just had a primary spiritual experience.

(I'd already decided what it should be called
and what level of importance it held.)

She needs to hear this.
I've got things to talk about!

I meant the being held in love,
the entire tunnel of love
and wondering whether the whole team
felt held in love
and whether we'd altered
the course of neurosurgery
by holding the team and me in love.
Surely this was all food for a Sunday morning
conversation with Krista while

thousands got ready for church.
On so many days,
I had been part of those thousands,
soaking in words from Wendell Berry,
Sandy Eisenberg Sasso, Yahia Labadidi.
I had something to add.

Florist

A man's gruff voice: *Is anyone home?*

Well, no. I'm recovering from neurosurgery
at University Hospital.
Instantly, I realize I should have screened the call—
but I felt relatively rested and was curious.
I did not recognize the number,
but thought it was no one
with whom I should not speak.

I've got flowers to deliver to you.

Suddenly I understand: He's a florist,
right now at my house
trying to deliver an order.

    Can you take them to my neighbors?

You mean just give *them?*

Yes. I had meant that.
Give them to someone else to enjoy

since I'm not home.

Lady, I can't do that.

   You can't leave them for my neighbors?

You mean across the street?

   Next house to the west.

It's hard to visualize
where the house is in relation to the hospital,
but the city, the neighborhood in which I live, is west of Detroit,
east of Chicago;
my neighbor is closer to Chicago than I.

People with the goose on the front porch?

   Yes I say, meaning not a live goose wandering
   but the large white-painted, plastic one.

Then: *Tell you what I'm going to do.*
I'm going to leave them right here on your steps.

I have visions of broken glass
and strewn tulips over ten yards;
someone comes at dusk
to feed the cats or bring in mail
and doesn't see them,
opens the screen door to go in
and breaks everything.
It's a dangerous mess.

But I get it:
My parents are sending the flowers
they are thankful
they will not be sending to my funeral;
they are splurging everything now:

See these! For you!

Nothing to do.

I say good-bye. Lie back.
The neighborhood will have
tulips blooming on concrete steps
in an elegant vase
for at least a few hours.

Without Glasses

It takes a lot for me to remember
I am not wearing glasses.
I am scribbling this as quick hieroglyph
in shadows well past midnight,
without aid of tempered and slightly curved glass
held near my eyes by expensive curved wires.
My brain is figuring out what to do, anyway.
I thought it would.

Everyone Says

Everyone says *You look so good!*
Finally I ask *What would I look like*
if I didn't *look good?*

Hell, I've just had brain surgery.
I have a right to look pretty awful.
I think I look like someone whacked me a good
one over my right eye with an iron skillet.

The orbital ridge under my eye
is guardian to a puffed collection of colored fluid—
little eggs of light yellow, lavender-grey,
and rose. The latter two are
my favorite colors.
I don't usually wear pale yellow,
especially as the bruise this so clearly is.
So I talk to the swelling.

I tell it: *You've done your work.*

It has come after the doctor—
whose passion is just this sort of
right frontal lobe removal of lethal intruders—
has removed tendrils that otherwise
would have grown to destroy
my vision, my memory, my *me.*
I think the bruising is just showing
how tightly the tumor had been holding.

It's okay to let go, now
I tell my sweet, battered body.

June 12

Message from My Neighbor

In the days since I have not called to say
I did not die.
I can walk, move my tongue, speak—

All I thought—blissfully—was
Marie is taking care of Hope and Eliza.
The cats are fine.

Your babies are fine Marie announces
when finally we speak.
First couple of days they were pretty freaked
but I kept going back and sitting with them
and now they're out and fine.

8:40 AM

Remembering some of the insights
from surgery:

All the little stuff adds up
and in the end is enough.
I don't have to start over

doing something big and new:
My life is already well underway.
Just paying attention
step by step is enough:

What do you notice?
What's happening now?

Nurses are eager to cancel any pain.
I admit to little
until finally Lisa* tells me
It's better to get ahead of the curve.
It's a lot easier on your body.

I begin to say
Yes, I do have some pain.

It has been more my jaw joints—
stretched for anesthesia—
than my sweet head.

What I'd figured is:
Pain?
Minor.
You got the tumor.
I got my life.
Deal.

*Nancy's longtime physical therapist

I am desperate for paper.
One of the nursing assistants
asks if he can bring me anything.
A pen I say *and paper—lots of paper.*
Can you do that?

He nods, serious.
He may understand.

He treats me formally—
as though I am his grandmother—his arm out to me
the way he learned in some etiquette
or dance class.

I'm not that *old* I think. But I walk next to him,
testing: Yes, my legs work. Yes, I have the stamina
to walk down this corridor and that one.
Every cell in my brain reports what it sees
in the corridor, out the windows, down below.
Every cell reports what it used to connect to
that now no longer receives it,
so it's starting something new.
I am slightly nauseated, slightly dizzy,
but mostly curious:
I never before knew
all this reporting:

Hey, over here; foot lifting; foot setting down.
Forward motion.
Talking at the same time as walking.
Trees outside are definitely green.

I notice the tattoo
down the middle knuckle of my guardian's hand: *veritas*. Also the
    mouth and eyebrow jewelry.

When we return to the room, he brings me lots of paper
and a pen.

Other stuff I know now:
It doesn't matter what shirt
you put on this morning
or where your body fat is or isn't.
God cares not a whit about
which shirt or how your body looks.
The point is love, which shows
just as well in your white shirt
as your blue one;
just as well, if not more clearly,
out of a battered body
as a coiffed one.
Cleanliness matters, yes—
but not how you thought.
In the first place is love.

Marie and I sort things out.

How are you doing?
    Fine.

You're not paralyzed or nothing?
    No.

This is three or four days
after I call and say

Marie, I've got a brain tumor.
Having surgery as soon as possible—
even tomorrow.
Will you take care of the cats?

Marie says now

They miss you,
but they're fine.
They're eating and everything.

Thank You to My Frontal Lobe

Thank you for
keeping track of equivalencies like
today—Monday—May 30,
tomorrow—Tuesday—May 31,
and how these integrate:
same patch of time,
but after elapsed time.
Thank you for quietly associating:

Okay, now the toes are wiggling.
Now the hands are holding up the pizza tray
without any drifting.

Now the eyes are looking
from finger to nose to finger again
in smooth coordination—

all of this a miracle without my doing.

Gary Visits

Gary comes to visit.
It is after my surgery.
I have asked for exactly who I want:
Gary, Victor, Brian.
This afternoon it's Gary.

I wrap my arms around him
Before he settles into a chair facing me.
He knows me well enough to know of other adversity I've met.
He comments wryly that I seem to be uniquely challenged.
I say I don't see it that way but may be particularly blessed.

I tell him

Gary, I was thinking so much about you the night before surgery,
getting ready—and that piece you wrote for the Thanksgiving service.
Remember?

I tell him quickly about my
"primary spiritual experience"—
my sense that the entire surgery was held in love.
Gary keeps my eyes in his.
His face is my friend Sam Dameron's at age eight.

Then, as I wrap my fingers around his on the over-bed tray:
Nancy, it's all love.
You knew that, right?

I think he sounds a little testy, a little exasperated—as in:
All this *for something you already* knew?

I hate to admit—given the level of harm and mayhem loose in the
    world—
that I am not entirely certain the sum and basis of the world is
    love,
but I certainly believe the experience I had during surgery.

Gary taps the tray-table
as though we have pinned the center of the universe there
and are parsing it out.

Yes I agree.
I know that!
It's all love.

Surgery Day in the Morning

My cell phone defies understanding,
particularly with an otherwise occupied, slow-working brain.
I have been wrestling for fifteen minutes
to delete telephone messages.
It is not clear to me whether
I have deleted the same message one zillion times,
somehow storing it instead of deleting it—

such that it multiplies profusely—
or my mother actually called one zillion times
and said the same thing.
I am trying to get ready for surgery,
scheduled to begin in early afternoon.
I have been waiting since Sunday evening.

Weary from the attempts to delete,
standing by the side of my bed,
I receive this insight:

Oh! I belong to my parents no longer.
I am now a child of the universe,
and belong to it, instead.

I have been distracted by my parents' calls;
have asked them not to call.

They cannot contain their worry
but transfer it across two thousand miles.

I feel suddenly free, lightened of the heavy weight
I carry: their insistence I notice them no matter what—
including hospitalization for brain surgery.
I see in my mind a monument:

On this spot, June 9, 2011,
Nancy Shaffer realized she was a free agent.

The insight contains also this:
My parents' job was to give me a start,
mangle me if they would;

then release me to my real home,
which is the far wider world of the universe.

I decide I will claim that release.

After Surgery: New Family Rules

So here's the deal:
Everyone gets on the bus.
Everyone stays on the bus.
We do the work until it's done.

Mike* gets on the bus with everyone else.
Everyone learns boundaries.
No one gets to be the star, the baby,
the dilettante, the power-broker.
We all of us work our butts off.
There are no other rules.

June 13

Fragments Written on Goldenrod Paper in the Hospital

. . . to do this on your own! The love surrounding me—
surrounding us—was so strong it was physical

*Nancy's brother

and essentially solid. I could see it. Sit on it.
that much blessing and protection
and fierce not-letting-go.

The question wasn't about
permission to end the surgery or not,
but hollering about how many were involved:
person upon person upon person,
each doing one small piece,
each piece adding to the next
and becoming enough . . . .
It's so much simpler—and also so much bigger
than I thought!
I tried to hold on to that knowing
until I could waken.
I was also clear:
The only question large enough
is how to give enough thanks for our lives.
That's the beginning:
large enough thanks.

Conversation with a Congregation Member

I have asked a congregation member
who also had brain cancer to come visit me.
He brings his wife and young child.

I am asking about treatment after surgery.
I want to know what is next—

when I get to hear the pathology report.

Are you ready to hear your diagnosis?
he asks.

Sure, I think, still naive. Hearing it won't change it.
It's not like saying it jinxes me.

I had called him a few days ago to ask
How do I start the conversation to plan for whatever is next?

Chemotherapy and radiation are next, I've been told,
but what does this mean?
Does it assume already some level of malignancy?
Luckily, I am in completely new terrain:
no previous conversations about
immediate finiteness of my life.

Perhaps overly cocky, I have been assuming that
whatever I've got, my body and I can handle it and thrive.
Besides, I am clear that the point is not
getting through unscathed, but getting through as best I can.
I'm up for *that*, again I tell myself.

We speak longer—this twenty-five year old
who already has faced some of what I face;
this not-yet-sixty-one-year-old minister
who wants to know what God looks like,
one of us concrete and technologically gifted,
the other interested mostly in the realm of spirit.

A good match, sufficient to the day's
and the evening's needs.

June 14

Face

In the glimpse in the mirror as I walk slowly
to the bathroom past my beached roommate
I begin to notice something new and good in my face—
in that smash of purple and rose under my right eye,
the stain of yellow turmeric
down the right side of my face
and into my collarbone.
My eyes are steady,
light-green, utterly serious.
I have become my own great-aunt,
someone's great-grandmother four generations back,
beyond the need for clean hair
beyond any definitions of young beauty:
old, elderly, well-used.
It's the noble part I hadn't expected
but which does seem present, unimagined:
simply what shows through.
I will have to wait, of course,
for others to name what they see,
but so far, so good:
a well-used face, well-earned.

Not one to flail in heat
or at a lame joke.
A real face.
Not Velveteen Rabbit, but close.
One I can welcome for the next twenty-five years.
A face with character.

June 17

Worries About Roommate

In the night I worry about my roommate.
Her answers to the questions neurologists ask
are fragile, not robust.

No, I want to shout at her.
Don't say _____.
Say _____.
as though merely reporting differently
could save her from
whatever her body is doing.
She has trouble keeping
three words in mind for ten seconds,
trouble following two directions
delayed by five seconds,
cannot tightly, firmly squeeze two fingers
held in front of her,
cannot categorize various kinds of moving objects.
When the clinician shines a light in her eyes

and asks her to follow it up and down and across
I can feel through the darkness between our beds
that her eyes do not follow the light well.
All this while she is only lying down
and they ask endless questions about urine
and feeling the need to urinate or not
and has she ever forgotten and urinated in bed
and when did she last have a bowel movement
and would she wiggle her toes
and hold her arms up like she's holding
a pizza tray.

I remember the pizza tray question from twenty years ago
when I had recently sustained a concussion—
my terrible anxiety that when I held my arms up to make the tray,
sometimes when my eyes were closed, my hands drifted down.
I didn't know: What did dropping the tray *mean*?
That I would never work again?
Never walk or sit without nausea?
Never have a full life?

When I pass her bed to walk into the bathroom—
such an extraordinary accomplishment—
I see that her mouth is shaped into the long, hollow,
    tooth-deprived O
of an older person who is dying.
I am afraid she will die before staff
can identify her problem and fix her.
The question is whether something new
has happened to her or whether this is something

she's been dealing with all along that now has intensified
such that it can't be ignored.
In any case, she feels terrible,
is very sick;
hasn't nearly so good a prognosis
as I—who walk past her looking
the real part: Yes, I just had brain surgery.
Yes, a tumor was removed
and look how I am still on this earth.
Our eyes meet only rarely.
I never tell her how sorry I am
for all she is suffering.
We have heard each others' stories
many times, in great detail,
through all the dark hours of the night.

Speech Evaluation

In the hospital following surgery
I failed part of a speech/language screening—
had not been able to correctly draw a clock face
and indicate on it the time.

Drawing the clock face I thought
*Damn! Why haven't I paid attention to
which is the hour hand, which the minute?*

I finessed the quick drawing—with that student hope
of all who seek to make a response ambiguous

so it can be argued another way
if the way first perceived
is deemed incorrect.
I did my best with the clock face,
starting out with a lop-sided circle
and a 12 at the top of a circle,
6 at the bottom below the 12,
3 on the right side.
But then I crammed in the 9 and knew
I'd not yet gotten in all those other pesky numbers
that fit between 12 and 3 and 9 and 12.
My head felt weary;
not like I had the energy and
desire for excellence to do this exactly right.

At the time, I had been surprised
but also not surprised
to be told I had failed the clock test.
I had been having terrible difficulties
perceiving the passage of time and
how to estimate the length of time
needed for a sequence of tasks.
I am amazed that the simple inability to draw a clock face
is predictive of such deep reasons for this failure:
Failure can predict a right frontal lobe tumor? Apparently, yes.

After I am home and learning
how to navigate my own house again,
what will be needed to put my life together again,
a speech therapist

calls to set an assessment appointment.
I tell her I will want to know
her training and qualifications for assessing my skills.

She takes me seriously:
In the kitchen, standing near the plastic wastebasket
and the shopping bag I have been unable to find anyone else to fill
and in desperation have at last made the time to fill, myself, with
outrageously decaying organic matter—
peonies, broccoli, kale, turnips, carrots, pears,
a dozen kiwis, pea pods, ginger, hummus, feta cheese—
finally throwing away decaying bouquets
and everything not frozen or in a jar in my refrigerator
plus the poor walnuts that had been soaking for roasting
and were abandoned when I left for the hospital
(their distress has made the kitchen smell like a dumpster—
so many gorgeous foods I might have eaten
had I been home),
she says:
You want to know my training?

She is slender with black hair.
Not much larger than I.
Earnest and young.

Yes I say.
What you've studied. Meaning:
What's your degree and how did you get it?

She lists degrees and the places she has worked in the United
	States—

A verbal resume, immediately.
I like her, right away.

And in my country she continues,
I worked in the ten years before I left
        with children and adults, both.
        I take the invitation. *What* is *your country?* I ask.

Taiwan! Her smile covers her entire body.

        Ah! Taiwan!

I hope I have done justice to her love for her land.
I wonder what drew her to move
and how it is for her, living so far
from her home.

I show her to the living room
where there is a table we can spread out on.
I do not mean to put her on the defensive
but I'm serious: If there is anything at all amiss
in my language ability, my life will be altered;
I want to have a very good clinician
be the one assessing that.
I tell her that before I was a minister
I was a school psychologist—
so I see my visual memory going,
see that I have some word-finding problems.

More than age, you mean? she asks.

I am still puzzled and sometimes insulted
when people indicate they realize I am older than forty.
Rarely do I experience this as a compliment.

It's true: I've noticed word-finding problems increasing
for at least a year. In retrospect, I claim them also
as part of this aggressive intruder.

She lays a first page before me.
I see that it involves categories and choices:
I am to trace from one thing to another without lifting my pencil
but in a numbered order
when the numbers are not presented in all the same way.
I see that part of the task is not to be hasty.
I pass. She lays out page after page of simple cognitive tasks;
I work with a pen to bring each quickly into sense,
appreciating anew how the ability to categorize
is the beginning of intelligence.
Partway through one page I give an answer
apparently not 100-percent correct.
She intervenes to assist.

Tell me what you were thinking she says.

The worksheet question asks that I circle one thing among four
that is different from the other three—
a mingling of concepts:
particular things and then how they are alike or not.

Tell me how they usually work she says.
I puzzle them out.

I can tell she wants me to get the answer right.

The categories and reasons I come up with
seem perfectly fine to me: if not correct,
at least bright. I gather my answer satisfies her—
either correct or adequate to indicate particular reasoning skills.
It isn't clear whether there is a right response to this question
or if it's designed to elicit conversation about just such reasoning.

I notice, working on page after page,
that I love this agile printing of names and categories:
    These things are _____ (furniture).
    These things are _____ (tools).
    These, articles of clothing.
    These, vegetables.

What a fine thing a brain is! I think—
noticing how my own delights in this galloping to categorize
and name and group. It is hungry to play like this.

The kindest thing the speech therapist does is
reach for my hand when I try to tell her
how important thinking is to me:
Good may not be good enough or what I had before;
there is nothing I know of more demanding language-wise,
concept-wise,
life-wise,
than creating a Unitarian Universalist worship service out of
    thin air.
It is a language-based, intellect- and heart-based,
life history–based work of art,

start to finish.
Ideally, the whole of it is woven fine,
concepts repeating and deepening,
spoken words, hymns, readings, silences all becoming one, new
    whole—
with attention to what the congregation currently can hear, in
    what order;
it must grow out of the heart, or it won't stick and matter.
It is nearly impossible to describe what it is like to make this up,
conjuring something whole and beautiful
out of ordinary Friday and Saturday living room air.

The Speech Therapist Tries to Reassure Me

You said you had concerns about executive functioning
she says *but I don't see any difficulty there.*

I smile.

Yes.

I realize it looks like I'm doing fine.
But: It's difficult to overstate how complex it is
to put together a worship service.
The thinking I need to do to lead that
is of the highest order of creativity and interweaving.
I want to know I have that again.

Tears trickle down my face.
She reaches for my hand.

I shrug, reach out for Victoria, who is also visiting:
time for a group hug.

It's true I haven't had time yet to grieve—
but more, what I need to cry for is gladness:
how extraordinary that we live at all,
and then on top of that that it is mostly such deep pleasure!
It isn't grief so much as gladness I keep feeling:
this extraordinary miracle we live,
minute by minute:
how I love it!

June 19

Limits of Psychotherapy

Cynthia tries to help me focus on feelings
but I am slippery,
fish-like, suddenly swimming elsewhere while declaring
I know how to live with extreme anguish.

Actually, I don't.
I could die from this cancer.

Having lived through a prior ending of my life is not of help now
if I place that knowing on a bright, high shelf
and declare its lessons known.

I am a handful, artfully declaring
I know my way in this new land while

clearly I am without a map,
without adequate watering from tears.
What I need is for someone to tell me to just shut up and cry.
Or someone to just quietly hold me until I stop darting
and let myself be found.

Cleverness has its limits.
Surely both can be true: This new land is raw and hard
and I know a lot about it and how to make it tamed, beautiful, real.
Because it has to be beautiful.
There is no other way through it.

So here's what I think:
Yes, Davis is the way to do this.
One bedroom for me,
one for invited, screened, welcome guests.
A year or more of sheer,
concentrated beauty.

A = Not B

This is such a remarkable concept in my family:
Look! One person! (This one: A.)
Another person! (Next to her: B.)
Two people (Both freely standing: A; B.)
Not the same person! (A = not B.)
Different awarenesses! (A= not B.)
Different, interesting lives! (A = not B.)

I lie still (one person, A),
not yet four days home from having
one lemon-sized brain tumor removed.
One person still breathing, thinking, writing
declaring herself one whole person
and the others intruders
who'd better figure out
how to do this remarkable, separate thing.

There Is This Joy

There is *this* joy, too:
The congregation and my colleagues *see* me:
They get it: The poet. The gentle one. The one who
weaves parts together.
I see this in their notes, the anguished ones filled up with words:
who I am, what I have been and done, they have seen.
Invisibility has taken a huge toll.
And now I find: I have *not* been invisible—
just the tortoise following the hare.

1

I wake in the night after deep naps four and five hours long,
feeling as though my body and brain have just accomplished
some great task of reorganizing and claiming.
How extraordinary this business of being human.

2

Slowly I find my way to several *No*s.
No, I will not complete a survey sheet of where and how I spend
    my time.
No, I will not make time for a phone interview for an evaluation of
    a program I participated in last year.
Yes, I will instead rest—eat spoonfuls of almond butter, spoonfuls
    of ripe avocado and fresh feta cheese sliced on soft yellow
    millet. Yes, I will drink vegetable juice so thick I might begin it
    with a spoon.
Yes, I will do this sweet being-in-my-body stuff: lying still, finding
    stillness, waking from stillness again more mended.

3

Is this perhaps true?
My body and brain have more time and space right now to knit
    themselves together
than they've had in many months, if not years?
Is this reveling in rest not simply *after* surgery but *after* an
    intruder's too-large presence?

Note to My Landlord

I arrive home from the hospital to a For Sale sign
on the front lawn. *Realty One.*
My landlord had a realtor contact me to say
he'd like to come take photos of the kitchen,

the bathroom, perhaps the study and living rooms—
if okay with me—and would I confirm whether
Saturday morning would work for me.
I did not return the call.
Saturday morning was not fine.
I was busy with a worship service to prepare,
also a brain tumor I did not yet know about.
These took priority.
And then I was in neurology intensive care,
waiting for surgery for a lemon-sized, aggressive tumor
camped in my right frontal lobe.

I did not call either the realtor or my landlord to say
You know what? I'm busy. Can't help you out right now.

My landlord's wife leaves a message
We know you're in the hospital.

So fine. Back off.

Finally, two days home,
beginning to get the sequence of cane, leg, arm alignment;
having cleared out everything that died in the refrigerator
while I was gone and every bouquet congregation members
brought in with love and set around the living room—
the peonies then proceeding to die with great olfactory
      announcement—
I call my landlord, beginning again to wrestle with calendars
and pens and the numbers of cell phones,
still not having seen my computer in over a week.

I say
I've just had major brain surgery.
I'm not quick with numbers yet.
I'm pretty tired.

My priority is my health I say.

Not helping you sell this house
I want to say, and don't.

Finding my way through cell phone phone-trees:
Look, you've got a perfectly good tenant—me.
Selling this house now is morally outrageous—
and probably (I rarely pull this card but now
seems the time) *really bad karma.*
You want to think this through again?

June 21

First Appointment

On my first post-surgery visit
I take—to show my surgeon—
my favorite get-well card:
a turtle on a luminous lavender background,
an ace bandage affixed with two clamps
around its shell;
also my favorite poem received
after surgery.
He reads the card and carefully gives it back.

It's the mending turtle shell I want him to see,
so perfect a visual metaphor is it
for an entered skull;
not the sentiment written within.
I am not sure he understands that
or if he thinks the words are the important part.
He notices both.
He asks if he can keep the poem
or if I'd like it back, now—
because, he says, he'd really like to read it.
I tell him *That's your copy. You keep it!*

I do not yet say *I will write you a whole
sheaf of poems about this journey.*

I want to hand him the one where it says
Look, you don't have to do this surgery thing alone!
Look at all the people helping out—
all the people I saw when I opened my eyes, after—
standing there holding pieces of love.

The one where it says
The biggest question is how to give enough thanks.

I weep, writing this. Who knew (well, I did) that living
right at the center of life would hold this much joy?

AnnArbor.com

I'm getting my computer back after more than a week
not seeing it or using it.
Julie* carries it (more than I may yet lift)
into my study,
sets it on my desk shelf, plugs it in,
then wrestles with the Mozy.com message
that reports I have been remiss
and have not backed up files in more than seven days.
Well, no. I was in neuro ICU.
I locate my file of passwords.

See Julie says. *Just put your password here—*
she touches a little box—
and then it will start the backup.

I am grateful for her pointing and deciphering.
I never *was* left-brained, even before this tumor.

Finally I see email messages lining up for my reading.

Oh, look! I say happily. *AnnArbor.com Local Obituary Listings—*
and I am not on them!

I read this regularly—
in case a congregation member's name shows up;
in case a young person has died and our kids will be affected;

---

*a member of Nancy's congregation in Ann Arbor, who stepped up to help her in
countless ways in her first months post-surgery

sometimes just for the old-time names
and learning how families tell the story of
those they have loved.

Julie does not seem to think this is so funny as I do.

During the night I wake up, get up, and begin to type.

June 22

I Am Still Mystified

I am still mystified by how days of the week,
particular calendar dates, and hours within a day
match and sequence themselves.
Even when I go to sleep at night knowing it is one day
and the day that comes when
next I open my eyes will step in
in some kind of repeatable order,
the sequencing of time can be a puzzle.

Turns out the simplest concepts are huge.

On this particular day—which I have counted out
as a Wednesday, the third such mid-week day
in this month of June—
I have fallen asleep mid-morning
with ice on my head
listening to Mstislav Rostropovich playing Bach,
gift of Julie.

Now I wake, thinking—as always—
only it might have been otherwise—
thinking, which brings tears trickling
because of the Bach and *that* I am awake, thinking,
and what may be the unexpected shortness of my life—
already much longer and more gifted than many others':

This is all I need: sheer beauty;
the chance to slowly, quietly, think and weep.

June 23

First Neuro-Oncology Appointment

The initial exam with neuro-oncology is pure tear-jerker.
I hold out my arms, squeeze fingers,
let light be shined into my eyes,
walk down a hallway,
turn and walk back,
place one foot in front of the other
as I walk a straight line,
say the sensation of touch on my forehead,
my cheeks, my arms,
my legs is the same on both sides.
My arms—already thin—
show off their reflexes.
So do my knees and ankles.
I repeat phrases and sentences distinctly,
breathe, gather categories together

(bikes and trains),
touch my finger to my nose
and then the doctor's
finger in rapid succession,
tell the number of fingers I see quickly flashing out.

I cry only a bit—
when Dr. J asks something about living in Davis, California—
because I have asked about the
possibility of going to Davis partway through treatment.
He wants to know how I imagine this working.

The congregation there I say—
and then my voice catches and I motion to Julie
to come and stand by me.

Dr. J points to the chair where Julie has been sitting.

You sit there.

I move from the exam table to this lower chair,
both feet grounded and on the floor.

I imagine people in the congregation
will help with a care calendar
I say. *I came out of that congregation.*
I went to undergraduate school there.
I have long-time friends.

I do not imagine driving myself to treatment.

I think this is important:
Others can be organized to help me
get to where I need to be.

Dr. J sits on the exam table himself,
a big man, serious.

We had a picnic in the summer for people
who have been through this he says.
There's a woman whose tumor we removed in _____.
Also a man whose tumor we removed in _____.
They were there.

He lays these out as gifts: *See, not everyone*
dies right away.

My eyes are fastened on him.
I want to know everything possible,
not just the clinical parts,
because these are numbers, estimates,
judgments of what best I can or should do
within a standard protocol.

The tearjerker part is this:
I want to live.

Already I understand:
There will come a time when
I cannot do the simple things they ask—
follow light, exhibit reflexes,
hold my hands out without their drifting down.

The question in the meantime is how much love and presence
surrounds all the changes, all the losses.

I realize that without my intending it
I have become a tragic, heroic figure:
the thin woman answering questions
with wit and clear intelligence;
the woman who—only a few days home from
near-emergency brain surgery—
has written a modest book proposal.
Both Dr. J and the resident who stands writing notes
take this in: a book proposal
in the midst of a very serious cancer diagnosis.

What fine work! I think.
They have the task of telling people like me
their time is limited.
They get to live right at the edge of huge importance:
maybe life, maybe not; in any case,
at the very steps of all that is most urgent and real:
our presence to each other
in this grand endeavor of daily finding
our way from six in the morning to ten at night.
They are witnesses to repeating desire:

Yes, I want to live today.
And tomorrow

and the day after.

Of course I cry a bit:
This is not the way I imagined the story would end.
I imagined I had another thirty years.
Well into my nineties.

Later, driving out of the parking structure,
I say to Julie
This must be a really bad cancer,
if they're pulling up examples of one or two people
who make it to five years or eight years.

> *Yes* Julie says.
> *This is really aggressive.*

We drive home.

The For Sale sign is still on the front lawn.
Flowers shipped via FedEx lie in a box
against the side steps.

I lick a spoonful of almond butter,
then go to change into my soft blue nightgown.

Julie busies herself in the kitchen.
I lie down to rest with the cats
and Rostropovich playing Bach.

Sandy* will come at six to take me

* program assistant when Nancy was minister of spiritual growth and
development at First Unitarian Universalist Congregation of Ann Arbor,
and now director of spiritual growth and development there

to my beautician for a trim.

I look forward to having a well-shampooed head.

1

Sometimes in the night
I hear myself begin to protest
*But this isn't the way
the story was supposed to turn out!*

But how do I know yet what was intended?
I know only as much of the story as I've lived this far.
Perhaps this is exactly the way it was supposed to turn out.

2

Every once in a while I think
*Well, I may not have to save
as much as I'd thought for retirement.*

But: I'd rather figure out ways
to fund a very long retirement.

June 26

Blue Bowl

One of the things I ask to have
brought to me in the hospital

is the blue bowl
Lisa gave me several years ago.

It is deepest, richest sapphire with a starburst pattern
across its bottom in pinks and purples.
I have cherished it.

Now I want with me several things that say *Lisa.*

The bowl is found and brought—
as though fired earth can protect me.

I am moved several times to different rooms—
out of and back into intensive care.
Several times colleagues and a few folk from the congregation
pack up my precious things and move them with me to a new room.

After surgery we discover that the bowl has broken along one edge.
I do not see this, only hear it told.

The tumor in its coming out I think:
The force of that shattered mere clay.
The bowl did what it could to assist.

Kimi* feels responsible that it has been damaged.

We can fix it she says.

From the description, I am not so sure.

*a colleague of Nancy's in Michigan

And: I do not want her to worry, but I do not
find the words to say
It's okay!
Yes, I loved it—
and it went to a very good cause.

After I am home and can talk to Lisa on the phone
I tell her what happened to the bowl.

She says only *There's more than one way to heal.*

Exactly. And I will take every one I can find.

I understand Lisa to mean *If the bowl's breaking could help,*
so be it. There's more than one bowl.

I admit that I am gladdened
by the very earth having responded to the force
needed to keep me alive.

Let the stars in their course be altered.
I will gladly receive their assistance.

June 27

Pathology Report, Part One

A week after the surgeon tells me
the pathology report
I am ready to hear it.
I remember he began it elegantly.

I had been sitting at the end of an exam table.
He motioned to a chair against the wall near his own.

Come sit here he said.

I did. Eager, innocent still.

I think now he was in misery.
I saw my poor head, my brain,
looking down on it from the top,
the MRI CD slices grey and darker grey.

The size of the spot where the tumor had been
floored me—bereft edges moving and collapsing together
as the images layered successively lower
through my head.

This is where it feels like it was
I tell the surgeon, holding my fist against my right temple.

Higher he says. *Higher.*

I move my fist up again and again.
I ask about size—
because the hole indicated by the MRI CD seems huge.

As big as your fist he says.

I study my fist; I imagine it tucked between my skull and brain—
where—having been told the tumor was so large
the left side of my brain was now being scrunched away from
     midline—
I had first understood the tumor was located.

I did not understand for a number of weeks
that it had knitted itself into my brain.
No wonder that after surgery my brain felt as though it were
a Chicago-style two-flat
with vines ripped off the tuck-pointing in autumn cleaning.

No wonder I had lost some things—like track of time
and some visual memory.

How is it that a tumor that large was removed
and I am still walking, thinking—alive?

The surgeon does not—carefully does not,
for which
afterward I am immensely thankful—
give me percentages or years.
What he does say as he begins
tears my heart:

There is always enough time to love.

Oh.

So I don't have

very much

time.

A body blow
to my heart

to my gut.

I had not guessed.

My hands in my lap are small.
They move to care for each other.

To how many people has the surgeon had to say this
always-enough-time-to-love introduction?

He studies the grey and darker grey images,
but I think he would like to roll up into a ball.

Who is the minister here?
Who the one in cahoots with God?
Clearly, the surgeon.
I keep my eyes fastened on him.

Later, when I get home and
begin to hear again Rostropovich playing Bach

I enter grief deeper than any I'd imagined possible:
This is the song that held me through the winter and spring—
the one I'd played in celebration for anything hard accomplished:
a sermon wrestled to written page, two hours of relatively free time
    cleared.

When Bach's cello concerto fills my room
it is as though I am entering my own memorial service.
Still, I walk in, change my clothes for comfortable ones for the
    house for evening,
and go out to be with the cats and Julie and eat.

Pathology Report, Part Two

How I have wanted to live!

I am—I realize later—in misery that first night—
but during the deepest hours of it, as I wrestle the question of
how to live through this even if
I can't live through it,
I understand this wrestling as perhaps the most significant piece of
    work I will ever do.
Satisfied, I return to sleep.
By the next afternoon when I have an appointment with Dr. L
I know what comes first:
living into my own wholeness—which is about calling, and which
    I am certain of;
creating as much beauty as I can—which is about writing
and also all other possible kinds of beauty, and which simply
    emerges from me;
and being present in relationships—which is about
my allowing my own holding of others and being held,
and circles back to the love the surgeon began with.
If I focus on these, I realize, I will live through this, even if I die.

A week later, I want to hear the surgeon's words as though
for the first time.

Tell me about how there will always be enough time for love
I want to say.

Start again at the beginning.

How did he come up with this way of beginning?

I think it was as hard for him to hear himself speak the report
as it was for me to hear it.

I had expected: surgery;
perhaps clean up the surgery with chemo and radiation therapy
(somehow I had gleaned these as possibly next);
and then as with breast or ovarian cancer
I'd get a number and a percentage and
move on to out-living the cancer and saying
It's done, over, finished.
I am three-four-six years past it.
I am well.
I am cancer-free.

I had not expected to hear grade four and that I have no chance of
    finally outliving it.

From the beginning (arrogant? confident?)
I'd thought
I can get through this.
I've done head injuries, for heaven's sake.
I know how to get through head stuff that's really hard

and that no one knows the answer to. I can do *this.*

It's just step by step.
I can do step by step.
I did not expect to hear that the nature of the beast is that
in the end I cannot best it.

Careful clinician that he is,
the surgeon says a lot about how *average*

doesn't tell much because
half are above and half
below any average figure
and I am not average, my own self,
plus the average figure can't include
what I myself will add to it.

If I had it to do this appointment again,
I would ask to hug him
and tell him I know he did everything he possibly could
to help me live.

I would comfort *him*
in this careful,
terrible telling.

It turns out my relative youth—age sixty—
may be to my advantage in outliving this.
A couple of other things, too,
which I do not remember.

Relative youth seems an odd potential advantage,
when the tumor could kill me
thirty years early.

Cats in Morning

This morning,
stroking their soft,
intricately patterned black and beige

and pale orange fur,
I have told the cats
I may not live through this cancer.

I want to protect them from grief;
I also want them to know why
I am so filled with grief:
no secrets—as though there could be,
anyway.

But I finish up, still stroking,
looking into Eliza's could-be-human eyes:
I will be okay
and you *will be okay.*

I tell them already
with whom they will live, after:
Lisa will take care of you.

They must stay with each other,
if they don't have me.

Then:
We will love each other
all the way through this.

They yawn, sleep-filled, languid.
Return to their beautiful poses.
I lie down and write.
They nestle against my feet.

June 29

Calling

I begin to understand *calling* more fully.
It has little to do with ministry itself,
everything to do with the Sacred.
It is not about serving a particular denomination
or even congregation
but being in the world who
I was created to be—
like standing on the stage of the universe
and saying Yes to God alone and not
a particular mountain range or river.

After that, what possibly can go wrong?

July

I might have died quickly.
This is harder, perhaps,
but exquisitely richer:
I get to grieve for my own self.

July 1

After the Pathology Report

When first I am realizing
I may die from this and there may come a day
when I can no longer rise from my bed
I cannot tolerate seeing in my mind that not rising
and how instead of rising I fade into another realm
in which I do not walk, think, breathe
but am dead—
I cannot tolerate that sadness of a last breath,
a final opening of eyes
and then my forever being silent and gone—
an image I know is real
but can barely make out:
real but much too vague—
such sadness I can find no name for it.
I refuse to see others gathered
and that last breath
because how in the world can I *die?*
But exquisite sadness pierces me
and I have to listen:
Bach and his violins climbing and soaring
and weaving themselves in and out of each other
while soaring and saying what cannot be said:
I have to see: Yes, that one lying still
at some point may be *me.*

I am reluctant to lie down at all
lest too soon I be the one not rising again
while others stand guard in support
and yet I am tired and must lie down
and so the image has no home:
One day I will not rise,
but it isn't I who does not rise
and that rising, piercing sadness is not mine
and the ones gathered around
are not gathered to pace my dying.
This is the closest I come to denial:
I cannot see my lying still,
my slipping from this life to another.

It's the slowness of it that arrests me:
not a quick losing of life
but breaths counted while waiting
and a consciousness all around that I am leaving:
This sadness is too much and I cannot see it.

This morning it comes to me to write my obituary.
I am surprised, but I write it—
even though reluctant to write when and where
lest I make them so;
sad beyond sad that my dying may be true.
How could my life come to this?

The same as any life:
At some point, breath ceases—
and the ones gathered see that and weep.

Then follow days in which my grief is so high
I cannot bear to be without those climbing violins.
I enter them, follow them, wake rested.
I say they are mending my brain,
but surely it is my grief they are mending first.
That soaring and falling and soaring and falling again
is not mere music
but my own one sweet life—
told in melody, told accurately:
Yes, there is a weaving, a soaring;
also a sad, sad falling from that soaring.

Primary Necessity

I begin to see that a primary necessity in grief is a witness:
someone who stands near me but is other than I
and can say *Yes, this happened*
and also this and then this person said _____
and _____ *said* _____
and the upshot is *Yes, you may die—*
while I'm resting as much as I can
and eating calorie after calorie when awake
and my brain knits together but
mostly my heart does in this new land.

Imminent finiteness draws a line around me.

July 2

Thank-You Notes

It's time to start writing thank-you notes I announce.
It is yesterday afternoon.
I have been resting with ice on my head.

Julie is standing in my study,
surveying the piles and boxes of order she has made:
files related to my work with the congregation,
a Trader Joe's shopping bag of paper to recycle,
a box of papers that have my scribbled writing
(*anything with your handwriting on it, I just put aside* she says
    without reading it)
a box of file folders, labels visible.

She has made order of stacks and stacks of disparate papers,
envelopes, files; she even found my checkbook.
This is perhaps the biggest project here: making order.

You mean thank-you's for things people have sent you? she asks.
Because you are ill?

    I nod: *Yes, time to write thank-you's.*

I'm pretty sure you can just receive those she says.
You're the one who's sick, right?

I nod, even though technically, I do not feel sick.
But I understand: Cancer is an illness.

I think people just want you to have what they send she says.
They don't expect a thank-you.

I nod, but I am unconvinced.
I am plotting when to write these.

Shabbat Service

This week, I do not weep all through the synagogue service.
Sandy comes for me a little after seven;
I dress quickly in loose linen pants and sleeveless top
and grab a jar of almond butter and spoon:
dinner I will eat as Sandy drives.

This week I can comprehend the sequence of page numbers
decreasing from left to right as we turn right to left.
Simple.
Only for a few weeks, it wasn't.
Sandy turns the pages in her prayer-book.
I turn in mine.
Sometimes she figures out where we are before I do.
It is helpful to have her example beside me.

The woman coleading the service with her husband announces
    that
one kind of prayerbook has numbers in parentheses in it next to
    the other numbers.
For the first time I understand the difference:
Oh! The lighter book is simply different in how it is compiled.

It isn't just my brain.

I had wrestled mightily: how to insert the parenthesized numbers,
when to notice them or not, how to consider them in the right-to-
   left sequence.

The prayerbook I have picked up tonight does not have
   parentheses.

I am safe: not this particular obstacle, tonight.

Before the service begins, as Sandy and I are settling into
how our bodies will sit in these pews, I see that Dr. Lawrence—
one of my favorites of the doctors now tending my care—
is walking down the red-carpeted ramp to a seat near the front.
I lean toward Sandy and nod in his direction.

That's one of my doctors I say.

I realize that, for the first time, I am seeing his real body.
He wore his white doctor coat, before.
I see that he is thin above his waist—not thick or muscled.
His back is angled into his waist as though he has been injured
and the angle from chest to waist altered, damaged.

He needs a really good physical therapist I think.

I wonder if he is in pain. He seems almost frail.
I consider: My life is in his hands.
I feel certain: *He is equal to this task.*

I wonder who else sitting here has cancer:
What do bodies hold that I cannot see?
That no one sees yet?

It is nearly the end of the service before Dr. Lawrence's eyes find
     mine
and both of us are suffused in a smile, eyes on each other.
Before that, in a time of open-microphone sharing about
Jewish ritual, Dr. Lawrence speaks of personal experience.
After that, the congregation says the mourner's kaddish.

Someday my name will be added I think.

I wonder how many of Dr. Lawrence's patients have died—
which is not about numbers but grief.
Surely he grieves each one, and brings that grief here.

Now—we are standing near the oneg* table—Dr. Lawrence asks
     how he did
in being understood when he spoke.
He had cancer removed from his tongue recently.
He is still working on how to fold and bend his tongue,
articulating words and whole paragraphs.

Beautifully I say.

He tests his tongue, twists it
in his mouth. He knows something he still wants to work on
before he leads the service next Friday.

I meet Dr. Lawrence's wife.

I'm a new patient of his I say.

> *Ah, he said something* she responds.

*the refreshment table where people gather informally after a Shabbat service

I tell her she looks familiar to me. She lists places
around town I may have met her.

No I say. *Here. I recognize you from here.*

I tell her I have been coming to services off and on for over a year.
I like her immediately: expressive face, kind eyes, solid arms,
strong presence. I know I've seen her singing in the choir.

Dr. Lawrence—sweet man—asks how I am.
I decide to let him mix doctoring and this time of after-worship—
his decision, anyway.

Very well I say.

I tell him that last week,
I wept through the whole service.

There doesn't seem time to add
Because it was so beautiful
and I kept seeing God everywhere.

I trust there will be time to fill this in,
if he would like an explanation.
Now I am smiling widely.
I know I look vibrant, happy, healthy.

What a difference a week makes I say.

I've had a week to make room for my news.

We speak of music, and how it is beyond words in reaching human
     beings.
He and his wife will sing next week.

Sandy drives me home.

I eat labneh on rye toast with sunflower seeds,
call Jennifer across the street.
What would you think about taking a walk?

We walk, nine-thirty to nearly ten in Michigan summer dimming
    light.
Fireflies light our way.

July 3

I Do Wonder

I do wonder when, how,
the cancer began;
what I did or didn't do;
how long it has been growing.

What else took birth when it did?

Colleagues Offer Consolation

*Actually, given our society, it's maybe
not such a bad thing to lose* Mary carefully observes.

I hear her listening for my reaction.

I have been telling her what I notice the tumor mangled:
visual memory—now strengthening again;

some short-term memory;
my sense of time and how I myself fit within it.

Busy as we are Mary continues
losing your sense of time may not be bad.
Maybe even a gift.

Because we know each other so well,
this is not a diminishing or dismissal of my loss
but sheer observation.

I chuckle.

Perhaps a gift to float within hours
without a sense of when I need to answer for what.
Particularly after nearly three years of sixty- to seventy-hour weeks
of constant intensity of endeavor.

David offers another deep belly-chuckle.

Nancy, he sighs, after one conversation about the tumor
and the race to the emergency room
and the surgery and now the aftermath:
This isn't fair.

He lands on *fair* with an entire chapter of emphasis,
so that it seems he is starting out to sort primary theological
      meaning.

Then—in the quick wit and turn of focus that are his hallmark—
he adds with perfect timing
Now *you've got all this great sermon material!*—

as though I've found an unfair advantage over hard-working,
innocent, well-meaning colleagues.

I collapse, giggling.

I'll trade! I shout into the phone. *I'll trade!*

Great sermon material
for an uneventful head. Totally fair.

Resting, days later,
I cherish the wit and love of these pronouncements:
Yes, a loss of my sense of time may not be a terrible thing;
yes, I do have quite a replenished store of sermon material.

Surely there was a less arduous,
less dangerous path.

July 4

My Imagination Races

My imagination runs ahead,
my visual mind already seeing
and wanting to know:
What will I finally die *from?*
What shuts down, in what order?
How long will it take?
Who becomes my main doctor, when I am dying?
I will not refuse hospice,
but welcome it and the Threshold Choir.

I will want someone with me so that
I do not feel afraid—
someone perhaps now unknown.
I tell myself I can do this dying, too:
again, simply one small step at a time.
This breath, and then this one.

I imagine I will see God at the end:
He will come to collect me
and I will know it and announce it.

After my books are done.
After instructions for the potential books that remain.

Air Before Air

The sadness of my dying
still arrests me: much too
young! A tragedy, given all
I have to write.
And yet I am clear: not congregational ministry
but writing as my greater, real
ministry. Even if I have thirty years more,
writing is what I most want,
my greatest gift. It is first language for me,
air before air. Surely it knits together
my sweet brain.
Somehow, may it and I outsmart this
most accomplished cancer.

The Big Question

The big question I wrestle now is whether—
if I accept my dying—I hasten my dying:
May I make room for it
without letting it come too soon?
How closely may I live in two worlds at once?

July 5

Power of Attorney

Cathy* tells me the story of how she came to the hospital.

*You were kind of high-maintenance for a while
because you wanted a cat.*

I chuckle.

Someone had offered a visit from a therapy dog.

How about a therapy cat? I'd asked.

Cathy went searching.

The people who own a pet supply store on the other side of town
have a large, sweet Maine Coon who was rescued
from a busy street near the store.
He looks just like Hope—low, sturdy body; wide-set ears;

*a Michigan colleague and friend from Starr King School for the Ministry,
who answered the call to come to Ann Arbor to be Nancy's local power of
attorney during surgery

large dollops of black on his sides, white chest—
except for being twice her size and plump.
A visit to purchase pet food is not complete for me
without a conversation with Pawz,
who now lives in the store.

Possibly the owners could bring Pawz,
but he hasn't had a rabies shot,
which they had been undecided about giving him.
Hospital regulations require the shot.
Also, he hates traveling by car.

Finally, Cathy brings me a caramel-and-white, soft, stuffed cat.
I plop the cat on my shoulder, close my eyes,
drift into sleep.

Later I leave a message for the pet supply store lady:
*It's okay. I've got a cat. Thanks for trying, but
you don't need to keep at it.*

Montana-kitty (named for the state a colleague is traveling in)
lives on my shoulder the rest of the time
she and I are in the hospital.
I keep my arms outside the sheets to hold her.
She gets sweaty, clammy, hugged a lot.
She sleeps a lot.

Cathy stays near, reading, writing, working.
Whenever my eyes meet hers, she is smiling.
I smile back, and sleep again:
Cathy will handle whatever needs handling.

Friday Before Hospitalization

One of the most Twilight Zone things that happened
occurred on the Friday evening before I was hospitalized.
I'd intended to go to the synagogue service
celebrating confirmation of _____* grade youth.
It began at the usual service time, 7:30 PM.
I left my house by 7:20 PM.
I didn't see the white fence at Fenton
where I'd intended to turn off Washtenaw
so I ended up going to Packard
and then turning south—but on Packard
I missed the left-hand turn for the synagogue
and went farther south than I'd meant.
I turned around, finally,
in the driveway of an apartment complex,
and went back north;
but when I entered the synagogue
I found the service was over.
There was only a custodian in the sanctuary.
My watch said 8:30.

I'd lost an entire hour,
and I knew I hadn't been driving that long.

*I can only assume that this word is left out because Nancy, precise as she
was, could not remember which grade was being honored, and intended
to check it later.—MMG

I sat in a pew for a time, glancing at my watch
and then the order of service,
but I couldn't make people appear again.

July 9

Edward Jones and Company Notice

Julie is driving Gayle* and me down a street
in the heart of Ludington.
We are on our way to Best Choice Market,
where the deli section will offer
just what we want for lunch under trees by the lake.

As we turn a corner, this sign,
written a bit like a poem,
catches my eye:

> How well
> you retire depends
> on how well you plan today.

I grab a pen and the closest paper
and write this down
because—from my new vantage point—
it's a lie
though likely good for business.

*Julie's spouse

If one retires at all
it will be because one was lucky enough
to live long enough to retire
and earn enough money
that one dares stop working
or has family who can offer a home
and one can tolerate that home.

Retiring has little to do with planning
and quite a lot to do with blind luck.
So say I, recently several weeks
and quite a lot of heartache wiser.

Which is not to say
I will not still seek to save judiciously.

The sandwiches are excellent.

Also the stuffed grape leaves, kalamata olives,
chick-pea salad, and green grapes.

The lake is calm beyond us.

July 10

Burning Card

Someone who cannot separate self and other
and in addition is often hostile
sends me a card that says
Alas I know too much about brain cancer

so unfortunately
I can imagine what you are experiencing.

I resolve to open no other cards
or even emails from this person;
also to avoid speaking with him.
Tear the card into small pieces.
Wait a couple of days.
Burn the card.

The kitchen smells of smoke.

I feel safer
even though—burning the card—
I wonder about
the carcinogenic properties of smoke.

Note to Self

Three weeks after I landed in the emergency room
and was kept
I find this note to myself
on the backside of a list
I'd made after surgery,
things nearly immediately to do:

Pay careful
attention
to lights and car distance, etc.
when driving

This is for immediate use.

I had scared myself the last day I drove,
spacey. Realized
I could be the cause of an accident
if I didn't notice a red light and stop
or if I stayed unmoving
when a light turned back to green.
I didn't want the last act of my life
to be causing an accident for others.

Now I wonder:
Where had I posted this alert to myself?
How did this particular piece of paper
end up with me in the hospital?

I want to go back and remember every step.
Not that this would change anything,
but what I don't remember might be made clear.

Figuring Backward: It's True

I am beginning to feel scared about
the magnitude of my vulnerability.
The big guns of chemotherapy and radiation:
These would not be employed
absent certainty of their need.

So: It really is true: grade four:
the most aggressive, fastest-growing cancer.

I understand Gerald better, now,
how he thought his dying indicated fault—
as though he ought to have found a way to stay alive.
His son was four.

I hate saying grade four.
I want no one to give up on me,
write me off.

I do not look ill, but—when not tired—
only slim and sturdy and vibrant.

July 11

My Neighbor Has Disappeared

My neighbor has disappeared.

I saw her just yesterday, early evening,
sitting in front of her house
with her husband.
Neighbor children were coming out of the house.

By later evening, she had disappeared.

I took some sweets to offer
but she did not answer the door
either at the living room
(television easily visible through the window)
or the kitchen.

College-age renters across the street
hooted as they played ball.

I walked across the street to other neighbors.

I add to this her failure to acknowledge
a call a week ago.

I went out of town.
Left a message asking just before I left
(I admit, last minute; it's amazing how time flies):
Can you look after the cats
for a couple days?

No response.
Later I left a message saying
All is well! Cat-care is covered.

Left an echinacea bouquet on her doorstep
before the car was loaded.
Some days before that I had left a note from the cats
thanking her for her caring for them
while I was in the hospital.

I think:
She has hit her limit on cat-care
or ability to respond, given my illness.
Or is withdrawing early, given that the house is for sale.
Also she may know from other neighbors
(who happily took all the sweets)
how serious the tumor is.

I told them.
She may feel hurt I did not tell her.

She had come over to tend the cats the evening of the day
I received the pathology report.
Julie and I were sitting on the kitchen floor
near the cat bowls.
I was vague, not able to tell her the tumor is grade four,
but she may have seen that in our faces.

Days later I tell Julie
I think my neighbor has had her fill.

> Julie says
> *When did you go over?*

Sunday evening.

> *Fairly late?*

She remembers I was at her own house that evening
until close to 9:00 PM.

Yes I say.

> *Maybe they were already
> in their pajamas.*

July 12

Day One: Chemotherapy and Radiation Therapy

Radiation therapy is not a piece of cake.

It turns out that because of its cost
the drug company will dispense only by mail
the chemotherapy that accompanies radiation.
It cannot be picked up at the hospital pharmacy—
which Julie had tried to do for the last two weeks.
I play telephone tag on this for several days
and believe I've followed every procedure needed.
The prescription does not arrive by Saturday.
I spend the weekend not knowing
if I can actually begin radiation on Monday.

Julie goes to the pharmacy first thing Monday morning.
She spends two hours tracking down information
from my major physician's nurse,
my insurance company, my insurance provider.
She calls to say: She's exhausted the possibilities.
No drug can be provided to me in time for the first treatment.
My physician says I should begin treatment without it.
I am hugely disappointed.

At the last minute an idiot from the prescription mail order
     company
calls me and wants my permission to charge me $25 per dose.

He understands no more than the FAQ sheet that he endlessly
      reads aloud.
He insists the supply I need is less than the number of days
I have been told the chemoradiation therapy combination is to
      last.
I am caught with him in the telephone loop from hell.

Finally I say, exasperated *Look, I've got to get off the phone*
and get dressed—I have been trying to rest; I am in my
      nightgown—
to go to the hospital for radiation.
It's my first day. I can't miss it.

He keeps saying the charge is per dose,
gives the wrong number of doses,
cannot explain why there are two separate prescriptions
for the same drug (so dosage can be calibrated to my size—
one of one pill and two of another, lesser dosage,
which together make a single dose for one day).
He does not answer my pointblank question of whether
the co-payment is per pill
or the full (and incorrect number of days) supply order.

I say again *I've got to get off the phone*
and get to the hospital.

      He says *So shall I send the order?*

I say *I can't talk with you any further right now.*

He says *Walgreens will bill you directly.*
He still won't say for how much.

I end the call, get dressed, grab the bag
with my hyacinth-colored sheet,
loose-fitting radiation therapy clothes
to wear in lieu of a hospital gown,
lavender buds, music CD,
and mesh bag of blessings
to take with me to the hospital.
Julie stops me.

Not like this she says.
Not so stressed. Breathe with me.

So I do, standing by the piano,
wanting instead to cry with frustration.
We get there five minutes late.
At the self-service check-in computer
I find I am not in the computer for this day,
this time. Must speak with an attendant.

When I am changed
and sitting in the waiting room
reading through strips of paper
from my white mesh bag of blessings,
tears trickle down my face
when the radiation technician comes to get me.
I quickly gather the strips of blessings
into my purse, but do not have time

to brush the tears away.
The attendant looks stricken.
I think she thinks she's got a real crier on her hands—
someone afraid
or just now perceiving the enormity of her diagnosis.

I do not take time to explain
Things people have written to me. I'm fine.

I follow her smiling, my cheeks still wet.

The mask that anchors me to the table
hurts my jaw joints and neck, and I say so—
but there's nothing else to be done.
A technician goes to get Dr. Lawrence.
He appears by my side and touches my arm
with both hands. I say the problem as best I can.

It felt okay when the mask was made, right? he says.

Yes I agree, which is only partly true.
It wasn't *fine,* but my understanding of
the best technicians could do.
It was the second try of making the mask,
which is necessary for holding my head
in precisely the same position each time.
They weren't set up to individualize for damaged
temporomandibular joints.

Now I find that my chin is held tilted up—
a position irritating to my neck.

Again, there's nothing that can be done about that.
A particular rubber support needs to be under my neck
to hold it in the position from which calculations have been made.
I've spent years learning not to tilt my chin up.
At home, down pillows scrunch and fill in
any tiny spaces not supported.
Not so, here.

I understand the standardization.

I tell Dr. Lawrence I think the choice is between
beginning, even if uncomfortable, and delaying—
which I do not think there is time for.

We decide to continue.
Anything else (like trying to remake the mask)
means a delay in starting treatment,
and what's most important is simply to begin it.
My brain and life trump my jaws.

Dr. Lawrence suggests doing only half the needed X-rays today,
half tomorrow, so that he can get the information
most crucially needed
and the time of discomfort is lessened.
I clasp my hands above my stomach and we begin.

Later, technicians say *You're doing really well.*
and then *You did really well.*

I wonder what I would have to do, strapped down as I am,
not to do "really well."

I am not sure at the end whether we have done
the full set of X-rays initially desired or just half.
Time suggests it was the full set.
When technicians asked me how I was doing
and I managed to move my jaw enough to say *Okay*
that was perhaps taken as the cue to complete the full set.

I memorize the three-panel photo on the ceiling—
a shot of a lake and sky and scrubby pine trees.
It could be the Sierras.
Someone has had the sense to choose as the central focus
a tree that is not perfect but in fact partly dead—
grey wood, bare, broken limbs with no growth.
It does not strike me as macabre, but realistic.
I will see it again tomorrow and can study it more.

In the dressing room, I see in the mirror
the mesh of the mask imprinted on my chin
in red and white.
My jaws feels inflamed.

I go out to find Julie, eat spoonfuls of almond butter,
schedule the remaining twenty-nine sessions.
It is raining lightly as we return to the car.
I am not finding much to laugh about.

Mary calls in the afternoon. We talk as though
she is right there in the room
and not two thousand miles away in Petaluma.
She remembers my birthday is coming in a month.

In the evening, Jen luckily says yes to a walk.
We take the path Aric and James and I
found on Saturday.
We walk near the river toward the park
where kids play softball.
Jen, too, has seen the big turtle in the river.
I show her where it was lying on the bank—
I thought dead—last week.
She has seen it snapping, swimming upstream.
It is—I study the bank carefully—gone.

July 14

Day Four: Chemo- and Radiation Therapies

I actually like chemotherapy and radiation therapy.
They give me hope.
I am excited to *do* something
that can send this cancer packing.

I had imagined I might speak to myself
remembered poems or scripture,
but simpler and more present is just to pray.
So I do, the entire time.
I align myself with the machine,
the machine with the tumor,
the love in the world with the technicians and my doctors
and everyone else who is in the building to help
or receive treatment.

And so the time goes—because whoever
has fully enough time for prayer?

So the time goes, tightly though the blue mesh mask
bolts me to the table.

You did really well say the technicians at the end of each day.

After the third day, I ask *What would I do if I* weren't *doing well?*

> *Move a lot.* The technician demonstrates, flailing her own arms
> and legs.

But why would I move?

I *need* rest.
The narrow table is relatively comfortable.
I have a soft, hyacinth-colored sheet over me—
I bring it each day—and a warm blanket
over the sheet.
Besides, the mask is tight, my head, forehead, and chin tender
where the mask pulls me down to the table.
I've no desire to increase that tightness and tenderness.
I can barely move my jaws to speak.

Sometimes I see the image of my face
in the round X-ray machine above me.
My head is a version of a stocking-capped robber—
same streamlining of features and hair.
There are cut-outs for my eyes and mouth.
Only I am not a robber
but one seeking to live.

So far I've learned:
>Cool my head and ice my jaws before and after treatment
and whenever possible over the rest of the day.
This lessens the tenderness of my jaws
and the old tumor site.

>Relax my jaws into neutral before the mask is bolted.
This way my jaws have the best chance of not aching, after.

>Stretch my hamstring muscles and scapulae
before, unobtrusively during, after.

>Eat labneh (balls of cream cheese from a nearby
Mediterranean market) mashed on dense rye bread
encrusted with sunflower seeds, after.
This is quick, satisfyingly thick and sour, filling.
Eat two slices if one isn't enough.
I get ravenous in the four-hour window.
The chemotherapy requires an empty stomach.

>The music played on the CD needs to be strong,
definite, instrumental.
Not harpsichord, which is too close to the pinging of the
machine.

>Buttons are okay to wear,
but nothing with metal.

>I can actually feel the beams of radiation
entering my head.
They are straight, intense, laser-thin.
Sometimes they burn a bit.

Sometimes the place where the tumor had been
aches, throbs, calls out that it is remembering
how that place used to be.
I can tend and quell this ache
by putting my attention on it—
calming my muscles and jaws,
sending the ex-tumor place restfulness,
sending it love.

Hair, Part One

I suspect I may permanently lose my hair
at the iso-center of the radiation,
so high is the radiation dosage.

I am fond of my hair—
brown with beginnings of grey, silky,
softly wavy, summer-short—
but this would be more than a fair trade.

And maybe there are ways around such loss.

July 15

Spiritual Practice Rather Than Goal

One reason I am doing so well emotionally
in responding to my cancer news and treatment

is that I have not just a goal (to write)
but a driving passion (writing).

I know how to write, well or not.
I've done it lying down for years.

I am not simply directing myself toward a goal,
but engaged over and over
in primary spiritual practice.

There is nothing that is not my material.

July 16

Nausea Territory

I have entered nausea territory.
I imagined I wouldn't or that if I did
I could walk through it
on the strength of what I already know—
as though experience
substitutes for current finding out.
I lived nausea for nearly two decades without medication,
just quietly moving, often resting a short time,
paying attention to what I felt inside.
Not now.
This is a different creature.

In the Night I Slowly Wake

In the night I slowly wake,
grieving my own death—
as of course I must:
I who so love this being alive
must of course grieve this abrupt
leaving my life.

Again I wonder what the final
days and hours will be like.
How able will I be, how long?
How un-able, at the last?
Who will be with me?
Where will I be?

Of course I grieve, now:
I can't be present and not grieve.
I would grieve any tragic death I knew—
and my own dying soon or in a few years
would be tragic.

What I think is:
I am well-suited to looking death
in the face, in the eyes—
well-suited because I am drawn in my living
to that transition point between two worlds;
also because I can tell with my pen
the story of this looking,
whether in poems or memorial service narratives;
also because I know I am held in God.

However I got this awareness of being held—
whether through surviving abuse, young—
I have it; it sustains me, now.
I do see this mystery:
The very abuse that positioned me
for this early death
assists me in living through its grief.

I Watch Myself

I watch myself move:
small, slim (as of now), sure-footed,
even bouncy.
Clothes like colors in a garden.
My very body is a call for grief:
How could this end?

I Want to Know How Oncologists Stay Present

I want to know how oncologists stay present
in the midst of continual loss.

Do they think *Maybe this one will live?*

Particularly for grade four cancer,
how do they dare enter relationship?

Because they must,
so the one with cancer isn't alone,

isn't only a name,
isn't simply a particular kind of cancer.

And how do I ask such an intimate question
and not at the same time be intrusive?

Here's Where I Don't Want to Go

Here's where I don't want to go:

Had I not been so terribly busy,
might I have noticed earlier
how terribly I was struggling?

Had I noticed earlier,
might I now live longer?

Did the environment I worked in
make the tumor grade four
and not something less aggressive?

All of these are questions of guilt:
What might I have done that I didn't?

All of these are questions of remorse:
How did I contribute to my own death?

Advantage

This is not lost on me:
Given that I have a tumor

that—I am told—will someday kill me
I have also the advantage
that I must reflect now—
while I am alive—
on the meaning of my life
and how I want to leave it.

I might have died quickly.

This is harder, perhaps,
but exquisitely richer:
I get to grieve for my own self.

How tender and not-to-be-missed
is this?

Day Five: Chemotherapy and Radiation

This was not so bouncy
as the previous days.

I began to get nauseated last night.
I was working on poems on the computer;
I thought I might have pushed too hard,
both eyes and body—
but in the morning, eating soup for breakfast,
again I felt it, this time proposing to myself
maybe the weight of the food
impinging on a nerve slightly strayed from home:
something that could be fixed mechanically

so I could continue to bounce.
I do want to walk outside.

But I am persuaded it is not only an irritated nerve:
It's the strength of the chemotherapy.

As I write this, Hope throws up,
leaning over the edge of her basket.

Honey Baby I say gently,
since she may have lost track again
whose body is whose
so closely does she care for me.
I'm the one who's nauseated.
Let me handle it.

I get up, wipe up the floor,
take the next pill.
Heroism lasts only so long.
I don't want Hope to suffer.

Also I noticed increasing tiredness this day.
Not the tiredness of not sleeping well.
Something with me regardless of sleep.
Also I notice I am not dreaming.
MayLyn commented on that,
dying of brain cancer in 1994.

Finally she said *I think I'm done dreaming.*

I hope I dream until the end.
I wonder: Where in the brain do dreams arise?

Aren't they a function of sleep itself
more than *place?*

July 17

Conversation with My Mother

I tell my mother I think
_____'s death
may have been a suicide.

Why suicide? she says.

> I am direct.
> *Because he molested me*
> *and also* _____.

But there was another man with him
she says—meaning when _____
began to weld the truck gas tank
he thought was empty but wasn't.
It exploded into flames.
He (the other man) *didn't die.*
How could it be suicide if there were two?

I consider this. Do not immediately respond.

> *Perhaps* _____ *suddenly*
> *gave up on his life*
> *and didn't care that someone else was near.*

The biggest thing is that I've named aloud again:
I was molested.

_____ did this.

My father still has not arrived—
he is bringing salmon he has cooked for their dinner;
he has his own condo but comes for dinner and the night.

My mother asks if I would like him to call when he gets there.

    No I say. *I've got to lie down.*

I need to rest without interruption,
without interrogation.

I hand the phone to Julie, as we'd planned.
I'm your back-up she'd offered.
When you get tired, just hand the phone to me.

    I say *Mom, there's a friend here from church.*
    She can answer any other questions you have.
    I'm going to lie down now.

I have told her I am feeling the effects of radiation.

Julie introduces herself.
My mother is charming.
Their conversation is brief.

Family News

Turns out that _____,
the one who served as accomplice
to _____, who molested me,
has cancer of the heart,
metastasized from the liver.
He's been told he has at most six months to live;
he has moved in with his long-time girlfriend,
who is caring for him.
He had seemed for some time to have a form of dementia.
Also suffered from hydrocephalus.

How to make sense of this?
Well, yes, long ago he did begin to have
a disease of the heart;
also one of the organs that filters poisons.

My mother says his doctor
(who knows his likes well)
said he could try chemotherapy
and add a few months
or go home and drink bourbon.
He chose to go home and drink bourbon.
His son came to help him move to his girlfriend's house.

But: I want no one glibly assessing my own cancer.

I think some occurrences have
no acceptable moral explanation
other than sheer bad luck—

gravity, wind patterns, the age of a tree
and that one happened at that moment
to be standing beneath it.

July 19

Day Six: Chemotherapy, Radiation, Appointment with Surgeon

The chemotherapy and radiation schedules are still in flux,
varying each day.
I do not begin a set schedule until tomorrow.

I am in yet another room for radiation—
this one the first with no photograph
on the ceiling.

Again the mask, when affixed,
is painful.
I ask twice for its repositioning;
ask also if the three points of affixing—
left side, right side, top of head—
can be done simultaneously
so that the whole of the mask
goes simply down, and is not pulled
even if subtly
from one clamping point to another.
The technicians say yes
to simultaneous clamping
but the result is no different.

I relax my jaws and neck as best I can
but there is no comfort inside the mask.
It is hard to focus on praying, today.
My thinking feels pulled
in several distracting directions,
the same as my face, head, chin.
My cheekbones feel raw
from the pulling of the mask.
Afterward, my chin is bright red
even though the technicians said they put gauze over it,
under the mask.

The appointment with my surgeon feels disjointed as well.
I am not on the same page with him
the entire twenty minutes we are together.
He examines my stitches and incisions:
All is well.

I'm getting my hair cut short this week I tell him.
Ahead of its falling out.

Coming into the room, he immediately said
You look a lot better than the last time I saw you!

He is pleased with this.

I translate backward: "The last time"
would have been exactly four weeks ago,
six days home from the hospital,
a week and a half after surgery.

Yikes I think. *What did I look like four weeks ago?*

I thought I had looked fine.
I did have a cane with me, I remember later.
I stopped using the cane weeks ago.

The last two times I've seen you
he amends, perhaps seeing in my face
the backward translation
and including in the two times
seeing me in the hospital post-surgery.

I decide maybe he means the *whole*
in that "better":
the ease with which I move,
my sturdiness on my feet,
my smile, a sense of my having reclaimed
my own body—
which I live from the inside out, now,
rather than as a stranger I am meeting
and carefully bringing along with me.

I pass the neurological tests—
which does not seem to
have been in doubt.

He is ready to release me
to a three-month schedule,
seeing him in conjunction with my oncologist.
I sense he had decided this release almost instantly,
walking into the room.

I had imagined I would see him monthly for a time.

I am freed to drink "free water"—
water just on its own and not added to juice,
the sort of water that has been my primary source of liquids
the last thirty years.
Each time I poured it into something else
and could not drink it alone
this last six weeks,
I had missed it.

I gather I will see him again
for significant help
only if there is additional need for surgery.
I cannot fathom that.

The few questions I ask are awkward:

What's an appropriate way to offer thanks to the surgical team?

Write a letter to the head of the hospital, he says;
mention specific people if I like.

This is certainly doable, I think.
Actually a lot easier than the meal
I had first thought to plan.

What conditions set the stage
for underlying factors to evolve into such a tumor?—
which is not a study question about tumor origin
but really—as I am able to decipher and tell him—
a question about my own part in its developing.

He says it likely is *not* genetic unless
the great-aunt who I think died from a brain tumor
died from exactly the same kind;
in any case, now I am post-surgery,
so my odds begin from here.

He also says it isn't trauma-induced,
as from the work injuries:
There was no indication of a concern
in the records from Medical College of Wisconsin.
I am impressed that he read and remembers this.

About it being stress-induced (on my end then
a point of profound personal forgiveness needed)
he says—essentially—no.
Stress results in other forms of illness,
but not this.
I am not convinced, but do not pursue
further questions.
It may be decades or even centuries
before a link is established
to the satisfaction of general medicine.

Almost immediately after the appointment ends
I wish I had thanked him again
for his skill, the surgery,
his care in bringing me through surgery.
I owe my life to him.
Instead I just said good-bye.

That night, having eaten dinner
and washed my hyacinth-colored sheet
and clothing for the next day,
I am unable to sleep until late—
the first such sleep-failure since coming home.

My head is newly tender at the bone-window site.
I try to keep it from touching
even scrunched-up down pillow.
I wonder about it:
Why the increased tenderness?

It could use new ice,
but I do not want to get up to get it.

Another Thing I Wonder

Another thing I wonder about oncologists:

How does *type* of cancer
influence relationships with patients?
Does an aggressive grade four
make it harder for the doctor to invest?

I'm not asking in general, of course, but for my own self:
    I want my doctors to invest as though I had forever.

Food Discoveries

What I'm discovering about food:
My favorite thing to eat is plain,
whole-milk Trader Joe's yogurt
spooned over frozen blueberries.
The blueberries freeze the yogurt in the tiny area
around each berry,
making a Nancy version of ice cream.
I would happily eat only this.

Cold foods are more palatable than hot,
from which I can quickly feel full
when I am not.

I really don't want to chew or eat
complicated food.

Avocados are not appealing.
Calamata olives are.

Thick juices can assist with getting sufficient calories.

Absent the four-hour period in which I cannot eat
I suspect my weight would be fine.
I am seriously hungry by two hours into the fasting,
from which I lose essentially a meal a day.

Dipping bread into olive oil
can help me add calories and good fat.

Treatment Attire

I have settled on my radiation treatment attire:
loose grey-lavender linen pants
and a grey-green long linen tunic
with a white sleeveless scoop-neck top
or other layer under the tunic.
I wear these from home,
go straight to the treatment waiting room
without stopping in the dressing room.
I do not put on earrings;
these are for after.
My sandals are fine to wear
into the treatment room.
I lie down on the floor of the waiting room,
stretch my hamstring muscles of my legs above my head.

In the beginning I wore other street clothes—
even earrings—
and then changed just before treatment,
but that's extra time, extra effort.
I just want to go and return home
as easily and quickly as possible.

Each night I launder my sheet,
linen pants and tunic
and the blue bag that carries the sheet,
my music CD, small bags of lavender buds,
and the bag of blessings and heart from Sandy.

T-Shirt

I anticipate (where does this come from?)
a sense of shame without my hair:
>Yes, I am not pretty.
>Yes, I have a serious illness.
>Yes, I am not thought to be among the long-termers here.

What an odd reaction, shame—
as though my cancer were my fault;
as though I am not worth as much,
if not pretty or trying to be;
as though the span of my life were my doing.

Perhaps now is when I need for myself
and to give to close others
the T-shirt I saw some wearing in the hospital:
>*It IS brain surgery.*

I could wear this on radiation days
and then add my grey-green tunic over it
when I change.

Hair, Part Two

I have an appointment two days from now,
very early morning, for my hair to be cut short—
so that I can start getting used to
how I will look without it.
According to my medication information,

hair begins to fall out two to three weeks
after the first radiation treatment.
Next Monday will be two weeks.

I like lots of hair.

I doubt I have the bone structure for zero-hair to look good.

The loss isn't so much *hair*
as sense of place among the well.

I have essentially been *passing*,
and I treasured that:
    Not brain surgery
    Not cancer
    Not any possibly-soon-to-be-definitely finite lifespan.

All of the *You look so good!* comments
from those I meet may cease
if what they really meant was *Wow.*
They didn't shave your head.

The advantage will be that
I can see the incision lines
and the remainder of the stitches
and can properly thank my head
for what it endured.

July 20

1:30 AM

I have been awake for at least two hours—
nausea, hunger, grief.

Yesterday was hard—
the idiocy of the conversation with the radiology resident,
radiation itself,
the appointment with my neuro-oncologist—
although also a gift and healing in its depth.

I am tired.
I think I might be able to sleep
if hunger were not distracting
and I could dare to enter Bach.

My thoughts are everywhere:
To whom to give what of my possessions,
what _____ might say that would signal to me
actual remorse; what I would say back;
the beginnings of a half-dozen poems;
what I wish I could say to my neuro-oncologist
that I didn't say yesterday.
The cats sleep through my turning on
the bedside light.

Twice Now When I Have Let Tears Slip

Twice now when I have let tears slip
or looked as though I might,
those treating me have proposed that,
if I would like,
an anti-depressant can be prescribed.

> *No* I have said, both times.
> *It's grief, and right on target.*

Well, we don't want you to suffer said one.
Well, if it lasts more than two weeks
said the other.

Actually I think I need more grief
rather than less I told both.

I mean, what the hell?
Isn't a life lost early
reason to cry
and cry without end?

I don't cry easily
but I do cry regularly—
or weep, rather: seep tears
when I am home
and lying down and thinking.
In the night or resting.
How could I not,
and be present?

About Regrets

I remember hearing that when Isao was very ill
and might not have lived but did—
he said that were he to die then,
he would have no regrets about his life.

I was envious of his sureness.

Years later, I have two major regrets:
That I did not marry.
That I did not raise children.

Both of these flow out of the harshness of my own raising,
and then the second from the first;
but I can't say I *regret* my childhood,
which was good in many indelible ways:
summer heat; living surrounded by orchards
and glimpses of both the Sierras
and coastal ranges;
vast opportunity to read, sew, swim, think;
my early introduction to Methodism,
Christianity, and therefore God.
I see the line of abuse that followed me
and see how my family started it;
but I can't say I *regret* my family.
I think my parents were prisoners of their own devils
and did—have done—what they could.

July 22

Day Nine: Prayer and Coughing

So much for prayer.
Until I get better acclimated to the mask,
I think prayer is out.
I am not comfortable enough,
not calm enough,
not focused enough.
I just want the time *over*,
with as little as possible damage
to my neck and jaws.

I may resort to an in-breath, out-breath,
in-breath focus and simply count:
find out the number of minutes
and simply count my way there,
noting—as when I used to swim daily
a mile in cold water and hot sun—
fractions gracefully completed:
one-quarter, one-third,
one-half, three-quarters,
nearly the whole, the whole mile.
Except *this* mile, entirely still.

Yesterday I began to cough
partway through the treatment.

I wondered—knowing the cough was coming—
how I was going to manage it,
with my head held down.
I let out one cough.
Waited, realized I needed to cough again,
so I did.

Later, I ask the technician
What do I do if I need to cough?

> *Like you did* he says.

I had simply coughed,
somehow making room
within the mask.
There was no whole-body participation.

And if I need water?

> *Use your hands down low—*

He wiggles his hands as they hang
near his sides—*to signal.*
I imagine lying on the bed,
dropping my hands down below the sheet,
wildly moving them.

> Or wiggle your feet.

Is someone watching?

> *Yes.* He points to two cameras on the wall.
> *Also, we can hear.*

We would have to take the mask off, of course
(if I needed water).
And then start over,
because we can't stop in the middle
and then know
we'd return to just the right spot again.

I decide quickly:
Extra radiation is a powerful reason
not to signal time out.

Standing now, folding the sheet,
I ask him more.

Who does this kind of work?—
because I'd asked him also about the machine
and how it moves over the bed
and how the bed itself swings a quarter-circle
during the treatment—
and he had said intricate things
that I do not retain about measurements—
Math majors?

    And ones who like physics he says.

I thank him and go change into street clothing
before my appointment with Dr. Lawrence.
The technician says
he will take my chart out to the desk.

Hair Cut

I had dreaded cutting my hair short;
I decided to cut it—now,
ahead of first losing it,
as a proactive measure—
so that when it does fall out
(it is not *if* but *when*,
which could be any day now
given that radiation began nearly two weeks ago)
I am not so startled
and haven't lonely bald spaces where there is no hair
surrounded by longish locks that are also lonely
because of the spaces right by them.
The good news is:
Cut very short, my hair looks
not just decently passable
but rather good. Ideally, it would be
a half-inch to an inch longer;
but it's fine—much better
than I'd imagined it would be.
Part of that is the expert trim;
part is the shape (not my doing)
of my head.
I never would have thought to cut it so short,
absent chemo and radiation.
I look more stylish now
than before surgery.

I have a quarter-inch strand, two inches long
and wrapped in the shimmering foil used
for sectioning hair for highlighting—to save—
a statement for later of what *was*, now.
When new hair finally comes,
its color and texture may not be the same.

The stylist began cutting in the back,
my chair turned sideways from the mirror.
Very smart:
This was not a drastic shortening
decided by sheer choice or summer heat.
I could feel the length left as she cut: not much.
She moved to the left side,
by which time Julie—
who had suggested this early trim
and served as my transport—
was signaling that she liked
what she saw.
Then, with me facing forward toward the mirror, now,
the stylist began cutting the right side.
Then more shortening all around.
Long, beginning-to-dry wisps and curls
and half-inch straight pieces of trimmings
fell onto the black cape I was wearing
and into my lap, onto the floor.

I felt like my head was hardwood floor emerging
for new owners taking up worn-out carpet:
Oh, look what's underneath!

We walked to Zingerman's, after.
I ordered—so fun to say just exactly what I want!
the staff there are eager to make anything possible—
scrambled eggs with sautéed portabella mushroom, spinach,
and asparagus; parmesan cheese sprinkled over all.
Julie drank morning coffee.

Here's the good news:
The beauty factor may be doable,
as short hair draws more attention to my eyes.
I can supplement with bright, large earrings
and clothing in light blue, light green, lavender—
already my favorite colors.
Given that I have in front of me
several years of little or no hair,
this is huge.

The surgery incisions are not visible.
I had thought they would be.
Seeing them—directly touching that specific skin
to thank it for its efforts in getting me well—
will need to wait until
my hair falls out.

Doing this piece by piece is smart.
I hope being actually bald doesn't wrench my gut
or heart.

July 23

First Radiology Appointment

Another time I let tears slip out:
I am trying to explain to my radiologist
why I want to write:
what I have figured out is the most important thing
for me to be doing right now.
I could write what I mean, of course;
but saying it—just my simple words
in the starkness of the exam room—
is so completely sad my voice catches.

I shrug.

It's about God

I say finally, meaning:
What I choose, I choose in relation to God.
What I want is to be the person I was created to be.
I want to use my remaining time for that.
I know I have a particular gift.

But what I mean is much more sad and poignant than this:
My writing is the gift I am charged to set loose in the world.
I have to meet that obligation.
I try to say what I figured out the night before:
wholeness, writing, relationship—but it is too tender.
I am too filled with grief.

Dr. Lawrence says yes to my going to Davis
partway through treatment—

But not if you are going there to die.

I shake my head, holding his eyes in mine.
No, I would go to write—
which for me is to live.

He nods—sweet, good man. I may go.

We speak of his synagogue
which at some point earlier—the first time we met?—
he had mentioned
and which I have attended as I could
on Friday evenings last spring into summer
and also this one.

I love it I tell him.

He looks surprised:
I am a Unitarian minister.

It fits me. The focus is on God.

I just ordered a copy of the prayerbook yesterday
I tell him
but I have trouble
keeping track of the left-to-right turning.

I will sit with you he says
and help you turn the pages.

Swelling

I can see—just looking in the mirror—
the swelling on the right side and top of my head.
It's amazing to me that the swelling is of such a level
it's actually visible—not as a lump
but one whole raised area.
No wonder I am tender there.
I hold my hand gently curved over the right side,
note with my hand where the outline of my head would be,
were it just the same on this side as the left.
Everything above that outline—behind my hand—
is swelling—non-MD and nontrained healer
so I think.
With my hair cut so short now,
I can see the subtle asymmetry.
My head was not asymmetric before.
Even with longer and curling hair I knew this.

Sweet head I say,
and go to get it ice.

Others' Discomfort

I'm getting questions about how I'm handling my news/illness
emotionally—as though grief ought to be tidily
boxed to one side
or apparent always.

Neither.
Some think I oughtn't make my way to each moment,
glad
or if I *am* glad
I must not be accepting what I've been told:
likely no way out of an early demise.

But the truth is: Individual moments are not
filled up with grief.
They're just *moments,*
with sun out, blueberries in a bowl,
a poem before me on the computer.
Why should I not be happy,
moment to moment?
A time may come when
I am utterly sad without end;
but that isn't now:
I've far too much to do
and I *feel* well.
Why should I miss this time I have?

Of course I grieve.
But it's mine to say how, when.

July 24

Hope Finds Small Spaces

I think Hope is self-medicating by finding small spaces to curl up in. She spends much of the day curled in a continuous ball, head to tail, in her basket made from vines. She is stuffed into it, really, but loves it, sleeping fast. She has added to her supply of curling-up places a lavender-colored oblong plastic storage container with sides and bottom in a lattice.

Surprise

Well, damn.

I've got clotted blood along
the main suture line I can see
(other lines are buried in my hair
at angles I can't see),
noticeable this morning after showering.
That line had looked mostly healed.

Plus it turns out the medication I took
for the first time yesterday afternoon for nausea,
prescribed by Dr. S, is,
according to the U of M neurologist on call,
not prescribed by their neurologists
because "it lowers the seizure threshold."

I will not touch that medication again.
Let me throw up a thousand times instead.

Now I wonder if *all* prescriptions,
including the B-12 idea and those for the rash,
must go through my neuro-oncologist.
I think so.
Thank God I did not have a seizure.

The clotted blood might be a radiation effect
on that particularly tender skin;
might also be a side effect of the antinausea medication,
which can have as a side effect
easy bleeding or bruising.
I've left a message for Dr. S on both the office number
and personal cell. I'll call my radiologist tomorrow
and also my neuro-oncologist's nurse.
I think I should have sought clearance
from my neuro-oncologist in the first place.
I'm trying to be curious about why I didn't
and not just clobber myself for a potentially very serious error.

Free Sunday

Another Sunday—for which
I do not have to be present.
A free day, for which I am thankful.
I am gradually working my way through
the organizing and tossing needed

in preparation for next Sunday's open house
of *this* house, where, through October,
I hope I have the choice to live.

This morning, eating and listening to the BBC
with half an ear, I sorted through
manila files of recipes cut from newspapers over the years.
Lots of excellent mixings and matchings of my favorite foods—
lentils, walnuts, good cheese, tomatoes, quinoa,
millet. I could part with very few—
because maybe someday, I *will* have the leisure
to meander the kitchen and create tasty dishes
for myself and guests.
Or perhaps someone will cook for *me*,
carefully perusing these files for ideas.
I know what I like—just as with clothing
and art. Knowing myself isn't the problem;
free time is. For the present,
I'm choosing to put that time into writing.

July 25

Oral and Maxillofacial Consultation

Here's what I fear:
Apart from what I can do on my own,
nothing is going to happen during this six weeks
to support my jaws during radiation.

I have spent the morning making calls
and responding to telephone tag treatment-related questions
and just received a message that the consultation
requested through Dr. L's office is scheduled for August 5.
Treatment ends two weeks later.
I had called this morning to ask for an update about the
    consultation.

So: The learning will be for someone
who comes after me.
Likely there will not be time
in which to get something done
that will help me, specifically.

But—on the sort-of bright side—
if I need further radiation therapy
possibly something can be put into effect
to support my jaws with that.

I am disappointed, but not surprised.

The wheels move slowly,
even though my sense is that
I may be getting expedited attention.
Certainly I am getting careful, supremely knowledgeable,
and even loving attention.

July 26

Machine

Yesterday I decided to be curious about the machine.
In what position does it begin?
Where does it move next?
How many pinging or buzzing sounds per position?
The mask was made more bearable
when I focused on the machine.

The machine moved in this pattern—so I imagined, lying on
    my back:
nine o'clock, twelve o'clock,
ten o'clock, eleven o'clock,
two-thirty, three o'clock, six o'clock—
visualizing a clock face standing upright
but sometimes with the head of the machine pointed down.
Then with the table 45 degrees to the left from starting,
nine-thirty.
Then twelve o'clock with the table 90 degrees
to the left from starting.

Afterward—I would have been game
for the session continuing—
I ask the technician about the machine's positions.
I tell her I am trying to envision what it does.

It turns 180 degrees from side to side.

I wish I could see it sometime I say—
meaning I wish I could see how it moves
when I am lying on the table—
not imagining this would be possible.

Here.

She turns the machine on.
It bends to the left.
I notice it is positioned high enough off the floor
that its bulk can indeed turn
without scraping the floor—
a detail I'd missed before.

    Oh!
I ask more.

    Are certain rooms reserved for certain parts of the body?

Because I see bolting holes on the table edge
only for the head and upper shoulder and throat area.
What about breasts and lungs and colons?

Yes. Certain rooms are for certain parts of the body.

I've been told that the room in which my treatment will take place
will now stay the same for the remaining treatments.
I realize in retrospect that the change in rooms before this—
initially I was treated in a different room each time—
may have had to do with the time of my appointment:
for about the first eight days I had an inconsistent schedule.

Maybe my treatment then was fit in
wherever a room was available,
no matter the time—
and then my mask was moved
from room to room.

I had liked the technicians I had initially;
have missed them since.
I know that technicians work in specific rooms.
I do not yet understand the difference between
those who come into the room and those who don't.

I ask for my Mozart CD—
I've settled on *Eine Kleine Nacht Musik*—
say good-bye,
and walk out the curving entryway,
ten feet wide and reminiscent of an airport restroom entrance.

> I ask at the main desk *May the technicians have fruit or flowers
> in their main work area?*

Because a half-dozen or so sit before monitors
in something like an airport control room.

Comes the answer:

Yes, both are fine to bring and are welcomed.

I have a new idea.

I have checked email anxiously today
a good dozen times for word of B_____ .
I realize the family may wait several days
before sending out word of B_____'s death,
but it is very hard to wait for news.
I feel surprised that the final days have been prolonged,
when a week or two ago it seemed death would come quickly.
I hope the delay hasn't been because B_____ has been struggling
not to let go. That would be a pity—
although it does seem as though the family gets that having as few people as possible
present helps prevent snags in spirit, getting caught in caring for others.
I will have to be especially careful of such psychic pulling, myself.
Just let go of others and concentrate on God.

July 27

I wake up so eager to enter my writing day
it is difficult to tie myself first to my bed
for icing my head.
Today I add my right shoulder,
which is much less painful this morning
than last night, when I could hardly
bear to move it—tendonitis, I think,
from typing.

I was up until eleven o'clock last night,
trying to fit in walking at dusk,
laundering my radiation therapy clothing,
icing my head, tending some emails,
doing the castor oil pack for my liver.
It felt odd to be up so late on mundane tasks,
but when I started each,
each one seemed reasonable.

Buddy

Here's an idea:
New patients—especially in summer
when there is no cancer support group—
are assigned a buddy:
someone carefully screened and trained
and who has recently been through radiation
and can see the experience from the new patient's perspective.
The buddy would have a sense
of what's most important to convey:
where to go, what is permissible to wear,
what the treatments are like.
It is follow-up support to the confusing
and perhaps objectifying simulation orientation,
which seems planned from the lab's perspective.

July 29

6:50 PM

I hate the double bind
my parents place me in:
Either I have no self
or I have caused them deepest grief and sorrow.

I learned this young:
To move out of a double bind
is to be thoughtless, hurtful,
the instrument of my own death.
I learned there is no safety, no winning.

Of course I would turn to God.
What temporal chance had I?
Everything around was unsafe.
Through God I declared the world good.

July 30

Anger Emerging

Yesterday I read for the first time that
those doing the surgery *knew* during surgery
what kind of tumor it was
and what grade—
meaning that both Dr. H and Dr. B,

when they visited me following surgery,
knew my likely prognosis
but did not indicate this.
I understand needing to wait for the pathology report
as certainty,
but what terrible distance—
to know and act as though not knowing.
Dr. S's office knew, too—
going into my initial appointments with the surgeon,
radiologist, the neuro-oncologist—
because the office had been faxed already
a copy of the surgery report where it tells the initial finding
and also the pathology report.
I was the only one who didn't know.
I am angry. I feel violated, made small.

What I Need to Hear

Here's what I haven't heard from you,
what I need to hear from you
if our relationship is to have
any chance of being real
or mending enough to begin over—
which you may think you have said
or is implied and I ought to know.
I assure you I do not:

I am so sorry you have been felled by this tumor.

I am so sorry this tragedy has visited you,
landed on you,
removed you from the life you knew.

I am so sorry you must leave the work
you have given your heart and strength to. . . .

That you are lethally ill and suddenly
pulled out of your life is terribly unfair.

I am so sorry this has happened to you.
How can I help?

Something that conveys that you get the anguish.
Something that conveys that you get
the magnitude of this tragedy.
Something that conveys that you get that
it *is* a tragedy. . . .

It is not that you are evil.
But if you can *feel*—
and convey that you
actually care about the pain of others—
then care.

August

She is not dressed for riding,
but she will go, anyway.

August 1

Family False Equations

Love = suffering

Love = martyrdom

Doing something "for" me
is doing something *for* me.
Their coming to Ann Arbor
would be doing something *for* me.

Caring for me = actual giving to/caring for me (vs. for self)

Setting boundaries means not loving
(*No* = I don't love you.)

August 2

Hair Again

I have decided to save the hair that falls out in the shower.

Because I sensed that Dr. L had noticed some thinning
when he looked at my head on Thursday.

(*How difficult will it be for you when you lose this?* he had asked.
Not *if*. *When*. He knew something.)

I put a white plastic strainer in the bathtub
before my shower the next day.

The following day I noticed wisps of short brown hair caught in it.
Also on the very next day.
Not whole handfuls—as I had thought might be the case.
Wisps.

I am going to keep the wisps in the light-green porcelain bowl and
     cover
from my grandmother's mother—a ritual:
I will gather them up each day after my shower.
It occurs to me to use the spray nozzle less,
which might be encouraging hair to let loose its hold.

I comb my hair carefully.
Encourage a hunk of hair to drape to the side
to cover the main incision visible, bright pink.

August 3

Sign-Up System

I begin to perceive the flaw in the volunteer
sign-up care system offered:
It's an extrovert vision of catastrophic illness
as an extended very bad cold:
Someone is needed to cook, to shop for food,
to do occasional laundry, replace a light bulb.

This is what's true:

Illness of significance is not
a simple lengthening of recovered-from illness known before.

Possible death is not a version of a postponed weekend.

A constant change in care-offerers is not invigorating
or even interesting.

Care cannot be contained in neat hourly boxes
in discrete, previously known categories.

Phone numbers are great.
But someone must dial them, must follow up to schedule.

Those who are not married or partnered
or possessed of adult children
have particular needs.
These are not their fault.
Judgment is not helpful.

August 4

Hair, Continued

It seems to fall out
when I am doing nothing,
only standing still,
as though it breaks off at the scalp line
or has from deep within been released
to another life.
I find it in singular inch-and-a-quarter straight lines

or slight curls on the rim of the sink,
the bottom of the tub,
the toilet lid, the bathroom floor.
The bedroom floor, the new stack of notes
beside my bed.

I wince, looking in the mirror:
My poor head is like forestland,
clear-cut of old-growth timber
around a necessary road—
all this visible from the air
and in quick glimpses
passing on the main road.

I am also aware of straightening my shoulders:
I've joined the club in which
it is no longer possible to pretend visibly
that I have not been through,
am not going through,
some unalterable rite of passage.

My head is getting more tender
I tell the technicians in the radiation treatment room.
Because my hair is thinning.

They are more gentle—solicitous even—
in lowering and placing the mask.
I am learning to find more room within it.

August 5

Early Morning, Early August

In the morning, waking in that long,
peaceful ascent from sleep into day,
I often now raise my arms over my pillow
to rest them around my head in a gentle circle,
one hand lightly gathered in the other.
My legs lie as usual over two soft pillows
stationed under my knees. My feet find
a spot in which to point and stretch between
the weight of the flannel blankets folded for the cats
at the foot of the bed;
then my arms stretch tall to encircle,
to protect, my head, which is still musing
in that nighttime realm of rest:

A lovely, long, whole-body stretch,
all five-foot-two and one-third inches of me.
All one hundred and one pounds.

Hope spent much of last night
guarding my right ribs.
Eliza took that spot in early morning.
In the dark, I tell the difference both by bulk—
Hope is one-half the size and usually lies long
rather than in a lump—
and by texture. When I put my hand out to stroke,
Hope is pure silk, Eliza more coarse,

with shorter hair, thick, thick, thick.
Both take seriously the task of guarding me,
which they invented.
Both emanate devotion.

I treasure this slow waking, this early writing,
this having rested well.
Night is one of my favorite parts of day.

Constant Attentiveness

Her constant attentiveness wears me out.

It takes me some months to realize this.
At first I think her only kind, solicitous.
Finally I understand:
The questions and compliments are inverted—
templates for the ones she would like told herself.
In the moment, caught in trying to be kind,
I forget to turn them to her.
Forget to tend the one who is supposedly tending me.

I need someone self-contained, self-assured,
emotionally grown-up although
always seeking to grow more.
Someone who provides herself her own feedback
and does not need constant naming of
how marvelous she is.

This relationship thing is so hard!
How does anyone ever get it even mostly right?

Radiology Appointment, Week Four

The general waiting area is filled with people,
some of them very sick-looking:
  thick, reddened skin,
  apparent pain when they slowly walk,
  swelling in various parts of their faces and necks.

I nearly bound, in contrast.

Do you need an exam? asks Dr. L.
You look like you're doing so well
it's not necessary.

  Do you mean lights and sensation
  and strength testing?

Yes.

  No. I'm fine.

I do realize that at some point,
my assertion that I am fine will not be sufficient
to ward off danger.

I mention the people who look so sick in the waiting room.

That shouldn't happen to you he says.
I believe he means the thickened, purple-red skin.

What arrests my eyes, my heart, is the slowness
and pain with which they walk. I do not—
cannot—say this.

I tell him that this week I cleaned out my office at church
in two trips, so that an interim person may have a room.

How was that?

    It was awful.

I mean: It wrenched my heart
to pack up my books and cups and water dispenser
and bowl and plate and pillows and mat and desk
and wooden armchair
and take down all the artwork
and take my gown and stoles
and turn in my keys
and walk out.

    I think in a couple more years
    it could have been a flagship program
    for the denomination.

I mean: under my leadership
with the infrastructure now coming to fruition
and the plans I had for the program.

Dr. L takes his time, busy as I know his day is. Kindly asks

Do you have any other questions?

It isn't so much questions I have or have asked
as a thirst for conversation with a witness
who can see the broader medical scope,
see what lies ahead and where I fit in that:
kind and calm medical expertise not my realm.
I consider but do not ask the primary question,
which only years and luck and diligence will tell—

Can you tell me if I will live?

Instead I shake my head No.

See you next week he says.
See you next week I echo.

August 6

Skirt

I've been wearing a knee-length khaki skirt
I got at Ann Arbor Thrift—
deciding to wear out what I've got
and focus on clothing I like best.
It looks really good, and
draws attention from my hair and face
to my legs and butt and hips.
I intend to wear it a lot.
I'll look for other short thrift-store skirts
for the fall and winter, as my usual attire
has been long and elegant, knees covered.

I'm switching to short and leggy.

In this phase while my hair is falling out
I'm also paying attention to having as wide as possible
a neck opening when I put a top on or take it off—
which I do a half-dozen times a day on treatment days.
I want to knock out as little hair as possible—
brave words about the importance of hair
to the contrary.
Now I'm in the middle of its loss.
I am aware of how pink and tender my scalp looks—
the remains of a forest after an unexpected fire.

I should get a photo.

2:35 PM

The tumor spot is aching, sweet thing.
The throbbing feels like it is
right behind my skull,
not within my brain.

I'm also exceedingly hungry,
and I have to fast an extra hour today because
even though I got out the Temodar at the right time
and even though I had plenty of liquid prepared
I neglected to combine the two
and actually take the pills. Julie and I were in
the thick of an intense and necessary airing of feelings
about how we are getting along;

she had followed me to the kitchen.
I discovered my mistake after she had departed
and I was thinking to heat more chicken broth
to divert and distract my usual
mid-fast hunger.
It's still an hour and five minutes before I can eat.

Career Idea

It occurs to me that I might specialize in spiritual direction
and pastoral care for doctors and hospital personnel,
particularly those who work with those with life-threatening or
life-altering diagnoses.

I might take the Bread of Life course
if it is still being offered, or find
something at the Graduate Theological Union and figure out how
     to get there
(or temporarily move and take
just the cats and see what scholarships I could get
as from the Pacific School of Religion).
Or maybe there's something in Sacramento
or online with periodic residencies.

My books would be the entryway to
demonstrating competence and credentials.
Perhaps this could be designated as community ministry,
offering at least justification for claiming a housing allowance.

What other kind of community ministry might I eventually
     engage,
after a year or two more of recovery?

Could I do this in Davis?

Sequencing

In the middle of the week last week
I lost track of days again and first thought
it must already be near the end of the week
when it was only Monday afternoon, late,
and then miscounted days and thought
Mary and I had two more mornings and days
when we had one.

Mary I asked, going into the kitchen,
are you going home tomorrow?

Julie had just said this was so.
Mary sighed.
I think she hated to tell me.

     Yes.

I loved the rhythm Mary and I had developed.
It was hard to give it up.

I am longing for this six weeks of treatment to be over.

I feel disjointed by the sequencing and time errors
I make. The concepts seem simple enough—

today, tomorrow, in two days;
then they flee.
I also still get lost in a hunk of time
and don't then sequence well what I want to do in it.
Plus my short-term and visual memory are still iffy.

But: All in all (is this just lack of judgment?)
I think I'm doing exceedingly well.

I've not come even close to throwing up.
I'm tired, but not knocked out.

Oh—and I'm writing a lot.

And most of the time I have a sense of humor.

Plus I've retained my appreciation of beauty.

I'm not depressed, haven't withdrawn,
am not wrecking relationships
but instead am speaking quite a lot more truth.

August 8

Horse Card
with thanks to Eileen

Another card, joining the turtle with an ace bandage
around its shell in perfection of image.

This one is a card-sized reprint of a Carol Grigg watercolor.
In this story, an Asian woman in a watered silk

long, light-blue gown stands mid-horse,
her head turned to face her right, where the horse's head faces.
Her body and her soft-booted feet point toward the viewer.
The horse—which is clearly very strong—is white with touches
    of brown
on its mane and nimble legs.
Its tail is thick, white, circled down against its back legs.
It is wearing over its mid-section a saddle of orange-brown,
a quarter of its own length. This is directly behind the woman,
so that her soft dress and body are framed by it.
All is forward movement—a journey about to take place.
The woman is beautiful.
She will ride well.

I can look at this a zillion times—a fairy tale of color and
    anticipated movement.
The woman hadn't been planning to go anywhere—her feet point
    toward the viewer—
but the horse is soon setting off, so she looks in that direction, too.
The horse is clearly made to run—gallop, even.
She is not dressed for riding,
but she will go, anyway.

Green Hat

Another transition point:
shortish hair trimmed to very short hair
reduced to falling-out-over-the-radiation-site hair,
as of two days ago covered by a lime green cotton hat with a brim.

I wrestle with whether to shave my hair or
possibly trim it closely where it is so thin
but I want no razor coming near my stitches—
black, rough, still partly raised.

My pink scalp beneath straggly hair when I see it in the mirror
after showering sobers me. Poor, denuded head!
I wear the hat to protect it from the sun, yes,
but also to protect it from others' eyes and their eyes from it.
It looks vulnerable, ravaged.

The hat is cuter than I'd imagined possible.
My hair falls in individual and half-dozen segments
repeatedly.
I leave its calling card everywhere.

Elevator Girl

Today in the cancer center
I locked eyes with a girl of fifteen or sixteen
as she exited an elevator I was waiting to enter.
What had caught my eye was the close-fitting cap over her head—
signal, I am learning, of sparse hair or no hair
or an entered skull—
and her age.
She was otherwise dressed in a normal teenage way:
white T-shirt, shorts.
I was wearing my new lime green hat.

She looked straight in my eyes—rare for a youth or child
in these days of teaching that strangers may be fatal—
I believe because of the hat and quickly interpreting it to mean
I might be safe—and smiled.
This anointing was quick and then over;
she walked out and walked on with people who surrounded her,
perhaps family.

What stayed with me was that smile:
Oh! Someone who is part of the same club!

I felt proud to be seen as safe.

August 10

Constant Question

The constant question in my head
is whether I might live.

I think to combine:
    Excellent surgical outcome
  (top neurosurgery team in the country)
  Excellent underlying health
  University of Michigan radiation oncology department
  (one of the top departments in the world)
  Not just goals but passion

Surely this is not simple *bargaining*—an arguing with
likely outcome—but

a storming of heaven to consider
major influencing factors:

As a good Unitarian Universalist,
a focus on personal agency.

Not Dreaming

About dreaming: I miss it;
but it occurs to me my writing
may be taking its place:
I may be doing enough processing in writing
that my psyche knows it can trust me
to get to the insights I need while awake.
An interesting thought (arrogant or merely creative?);
but I'd rather also have dreams.
I suspect the lack is medication-related—
possibly a side effect of medication
unremarked on before.

Art and Stories

Here's another patient support idea:
Instead of close-ups of bright and unremarkable flowers
and the television showing a continuous loop of nature scenes—
why not prints of actual, high-quality art
or quilts
that invite patients into a partly begun,

multifaceted *story*—visual fairy tales
to which they may add their own particulars.

In addition to magazines that may not know a meeting place
with a patient's actual situation (too ill to read much
or to read small print; not going to live much longer
so world events and summer recipes
and celebrity marriages hold no interest or never did)—
and because of this lack of meeting,
inadvertently discourage and separate—
how about a scattering of really good books
usually thought to be for children
but which people of all ages recognize as timeless
and enter with glee—gentle, daily stories
as well as collections from many cultures:
Buddhist, Chinese, Jewish, Appalachian.
Short or longer stories with evocative pictures:
again, something entered on a multitude of levels,
and different levels at different times.
Gently, humanly funny stories.
Metaphors that assure:
This (suffering, too-soon dying,
longing without chance of fulfillment)
has happened before,
it will happen again,
and look at what still might be found!

Or, more easily and simply:
boxes of laminated pictures and photos
and greeting card faces that patients can sort

to find the images that speak to them that day—
like the collection I use for classes
in *Introduction to Our Faith* and
Writing as Spiritual Practice;
images that show hope, grief, family traditions.
Metaphors of connection and stillness.

For further support:
How about a therapist or counselor
who sits in the treatment waiting room,
welcomes patients,
is available for inviting them into displayed art, books,
the picture collection?
What if this vulnerable waiting time were used for caring for
psychic health?

More:
a portable Zen sand garden with nearby bowls of stones
or shells to hold or place,
the natural world present in tactile, sensual form;
flowers to smell, sand to rake or touch, stones to hold.
A finger labyrinth. A bowl of rosaries or separate, beautiful beads.
Bowls of tiny pine cones in winter.
Stands of bush or tree berries in fall.
Eggs—undyed—in spring.
Plates of zucchinis and tomatoes:
the simple and colorful and easy to find.
Things that remind: The body is good,
knows pleasure, is worth caring for.

August 13

I No Longer Bounce

I no longer bounce—
since Monday of almost two weeks ago
because of nausea
and since Wednesday of almost two weeks ago
because of fatigue,
and also, I suspect, low-level dizziness
induced by medications.
I navigate carefully, slowly—
almost like an old person
unsure of terrain,
energy, limbs.
I bend with great care for my head,
which has increased tenderness and pain
where the tumor was—
where the radiation is aimed.
Once lying down, even if hungry
or I want coolness for my head,
I rarely rise:
too much effort.
I would rather lie still.

Turns out I am human—
as susceptible as others
to the effects of this aggressive program.
I still believe I can make it through it,

but am surprised yet again not to sail
but be subject to parameters offered others
as expected guidelines.

August 15

9:35 PM

Since that Saturday unstoppable throwing up,
I am little motivated to cool my sweet head.
The effort feels too much;
God forbid I feel that sick again—
six upheavals in fewer than two hours.
I sense I wasn't mindful enough and coolness
led my vagus nerve into irritation.
And then I wasn't able to keep my head up
when I reached down for something on the floor.
Looking actually down was the kiss of death.

On Saturday I misjudged my nausea as a couple levels lower than
     actual
and also the acute tenderness in my head on Thursday
as I walked twenty feet from the car to a store
shortly after radiation.
I winced in pain at each step,
though my walking was smooth.
I wasn't jolting myself;
wasn't being jostled;
was only walking on even ground

with a step up from asphalt to sidewalk.
That tenderness was my cue
the swelling had gone too high.
I might have requested help the next day;
I didn't equate tenderness with swelling
or realize a medication change might help reduce
the second and thereby the first.
Also, when I have reported pain in the old tumor site,
no one has seemed to give this importance.

I am much more comfortable now—
and also wiser.

No food heroics—
no cutting and steaming vegetables,
not even bringing water to boil
and then adding frozen vegetables.
I will gladly eat them if someone else cooks,
but not if I must leave bed and stand, in order to do it.
I prefer then not to eat,
hungry though I am.
The main thing is simply to maintain my weight
and not throw up.
If that means no veggies for a time,
so be it—because I'm not interested in
cooking them earlier in the day, either.

I'd like a half-glass of very good wine in the evening, instead:
fermented grapes as veggies.

I want to read or see someone else's story:
a mystery, a romance, a comedy—
respite from my own.
I've no interest in reading something technical or because
I need to know it for church systems.
I want tales, suspense that belongs to someone else—
well-written,
so that I'm not imbibing faulty style
along with plot.

And actually not so much poetry, now, as something
I can just fall into:
no taxing thinking—
just the sheer pleasure of a well-told journey.

Good children's books will do;
great pictures are welcomed.
Neither my eyes nor my brain can handle hours of tiny complexity,
but my psyche needs escape.

Thank God for public libraries.

August 16

Vine and Fig Tree

Another dear card: the song
Vine and Fig Tree
as a 4 x 7-inch quilt.

The quilt features an orange-yellow sun
on a square of brilliant blue sky;
a strip of kelly green rickrack
vining across the bottom,
and on the left,
a fig tree with leaves and branches against
tiny yellow stars in blue sky.
There are also a green meadow with discernable blades of grass,
more swirling leaves
and a blue-black button fig.
The fabric is stitched directly onto the card face.
A hand-printed edging along the left side and bottom
begins to sing

And every one 'neath a vine and fig
tree shall live in peace and unafraid.

The note inside tells me that during worship
last Sunday when this hymn was sung,
Rev. Gail announced it as one of my favorites.
It is!
Because of its anchoring in ancient Judeo-Christian text;
because of the vision it offers of shared peace as beginning with
     good and shared food—
delicacies grown freely under the land's sky
and then eaten during evening breezes, speaking quietly of the day.
I know in my bones what it is to live with grapevines
and fig trees grown as common garden plants.
My bones and eyes understand the seasons through fruits like
     these.

So yes, it is one of my favorite hymns—
perhaps especially living now where winter is king.

And here's the neat thing about being remembered on Sunday
        morning
at that hour:
I was finally then sleeping in my own bed
after an evening and night in the emergency room with nausea so
        high
I'd not been able to stop throwing up the afternoon before.
I was blessedly sleeping
while the congregation was singing what I love.

Vine and Fig Tree is a song I'd picked for the kids to learn
this summer, so the congregation would have sung it
during the opening minutes of worship,
while the kids and their teachers were still there—
and then the kids would have learned more about it during class.

The green rickrack is from the pack the card maker
brought to a Coming-of-Age stole-making event
a year and a half ago. It remained unused.
She had said I might keep it,
and so I had, but no reason to open the package
presented itself.
I had saved it, and when cleaning out my office
three weeks ago had asked that it be returned to her.

And so the loop has been continued.

I will frame the card—already treasure it;
I will be reminded each time I see it of its maker's
creativity and love
and the eons-long yearning for peace.

You Look So Good

Someone who hasn't seen me since the hospital says

You look so good!

The truth is:
I've lost three-fourths of the hair
on the right side of my head
and have a four-inch L-shaped scar that travels
directly down the center of my skull
and then goes down the right side to just barely
above my ear—and still some black stitches,
more noticeable
now that my pink scalp shows through swaths of thinning
or zero hair
and *all* of my hair is shorter than you've ever seen it,
and I might be darned tired and look it
and not be smiling
especially if it is the end of the day rather than
the beginning and I'm not wearing my jaunty lime-green hat
but still wearing my shapeless, comfortable light-green tunic
and wide lavender linen pants—radiation therapy get-up
so I don't have to change into a gown—

and I might be feeling pretty nauseated or unsteady
from medication and radiation—
so tell me:
Do you mean:

Wow! I can still tell who you are!?

*Wow! You must be able to eat! You haven't lost a hundred and fifty
    pounds!?*

*Wow! You walk, climb stairs, open doors, speak in complete sentences
    with correct verb tense!?*

Wow! You're still alive!

Tell me: What would *not* looking good look like?
Care to go there? What would you say then?

August 17

What's Your Prognosis?

Twice in two days someone has asked me
in a hearty tone of voice

So, what's your prognosis?—

as though publicly and quickly
naming potential longevity
is as commonplace as telling what one just ate for lunch
or where one traveled on vacation—and as easily engaged.

Or that it's like a city league-baseball score or golf handicap: not
    the full and finite you.

I realize I am beginning to look weary and walk wearily but—

Whoa!

That I am friendly and you know I have cancer
does not give you permission to ask
intimate details of my life.

I admit: I did ask someone where *his* scars were—
but I thought he'd had brain cancer—scars therefore quite open
    to sun.

My doctors haven't said I say.
They treat each person as an individual—
me included.

A woman and her daughter nod:
Yes, this is smart.

The woman is called away before I can ask back

What is your *prognosis?*

I hope I see her again. I shall remind her of the conversation
and say I want a chance to ask this question, also.

Might be the best way to offer correction.

She was a handful—
but I figure good practice for
managing other handfuls.

August 18

So What's Your Prognosis? Revisited

Julie wryly points out that the response to the
hearty but rude

So what's your prognosis?

may helpfully be a hearty

Same as yours: eventual death;
but a potentially rich time before that!

delivered without a flicker of eyelash.

She is driving me home from radiation therapy Day Twenty-Seven.
The road curves through lush summer shrub and tree growth—
sixty shades of green, eighteen hundred ten variations of sunlight
    on green
on each side.

She herself tried this once with someone—
spur of the moment—
and was rewarded with a sputtering, full-belly chuckle
and slapping of thighs.

I'm eager to try this out—not for the question
but teaching the response.

August 23

Prognosis in the Night

Again the question from a visitor—
this time a bit more delicately phrased
but still the same question:
How long have I been told
I may expect to live?

It takes my breath away.

This time the visitor knows someone else—still living—
who had surgery and follow-up treatment for a brain tumor
and was told fifteen months
and now it's two and a half years later.
The visitor wonders if my tumor and diagnosis are similar.
Again I am enormously grateful to my doctors that they gave no
    months, no years.
Which gratefulness I say.
My life and my response become my own.

But the deeper question I ought ask back is
What does number of months or years mean *to you?*
How do you take that?
That is: *How is this* your *business?*
which I do not, equally rudely, ask.

I must get up my nerve for the next questioner.

It's *all* pastoral care, regardless of what the visitor thinks
or intends. How impossible, of course, early on to tend
both another's grief and my own,
especially when weak and disoriented and in pain from surgery.
Or even now.

Envy not the minister, sick!

August 24

Sorting After Radiation

How *physical* this recovery is—not just my sweet body, as though it
    ever could be separate,
but mind-body, body-mind as one complete whole.
In these precious first days of no hospital, no radiation schedule,
    no extra tiredness and nausea,
I pick my way through one small task after another,
organizing my life and saying thank you,
noticing the crumb trail of what next opens what else.
Doing the physical moves me to a new awareness and receptivity—
nothing I could just say I need to do or write myself into.
I must physically engage the tasks and let them lead me one to
    another.

I delight in *what* it is my psyche asks:
to make thanks concretely known now.

I delight also in the accomplishment of the physical sorting in an
    initial once-over.
At some point soon I will move from this house, temporarily or not,
desired move or not;
and what need I take?

It calms me to sort and put in bags and boxes:
this for Kiwanis, this for the office, this for Sandy and the program,
    this for Gail,
this to recycle.
I also think in terms of just putting out for taking by people who
    have been kind:

I notice that for each precious thing I will not take, I want a good
    home:

Here, this needs a home. Would you like it?

At some point of course, I will have to let go of the careful placing
and just give.

August 25

Conversation with OTS*

I know quite a lot about psychic need in recovery and healing
from serious illness—some newly learned,
some extrapolated from my head injury period.

* Old Tumor Site —MMG

I walk sure-footed in this:
School psychology
Ministry in various forms with many ages
in many regions of our country
My own medical and life history
Spiritual practice
Spiritual bent

It's still relatively unbelievable to me
to say I myself have cancer.
I *had* a tumor.
Now I don't.
The tumor was cancerous.
My body is not.

Might be splitting hairs.

The OTS aches as I write this.
Wonder what it wants to say:
Look, I'm doing my best,
but I'm under fluid here, and
these cancer cells will at some point grow
again.

I have other plans: They will not.

They will disappear from my body.
I will help them leave.
So will others help them leave.

August 26

Fuzziness

The lack of completion this winter-spring was cluttering my brain:
a zillion tiny details that just needed time for innocent tending.
Untended, they formed fuzziness throughout my synapses
and hurt my eyes.

I see now I had at least two major struggles:
lack of time for personal order-making;
impaired ability to succinctly reveal essence.
These two combined were a powerful destroyer of
my usual concise interweaving of disparate parts
into a creative whole—
a hallmark of my work.

Reorganizing

This reorganizing of my life is utterly physical and sensory:
each of ten pieces of paper
suggesting what I might do,
am doing,
might best next do.

Pleasure is a check mark: Done!

Just the hanging of two wall clocks takes a shopping trip
and then trips upstairs into the storage cupboard
requiring removal of packed-away pillows and blankets

and into the storage cupboard to the side of the stove, lowest shelf:
screwdriver, batteries, hammer, picture hangers, thin ribbon.
Then taping the plaster wall over the spot where I intend to strike
    the nail;
standing tall enough on the step stool that I can
hold the nail at just the right angle as I hammer it;
hanging the clock and stepping back to approve;
setting the time and resetting after I've put the battery in backward
and the clock hand declines to advance.

And then the glorious satisfaction:
two understated, high-hung wall clocks that blend well with
    furnishings and artwork,
add unobtrusive beauty,
and walk me room through room
through the sense of time I used to sense exquisitely accurately
from any wondering
day or night.
I want that exquisite sense of passage and my place within it again.

The new wall clocks will help with that:

Now it's 9:05.

Now it's 9:06.

Now it's 9:08.

My doctor had wondered whether I might simply lift my wrist
and bring my watch close to my eyes.

I'd like it more like a newsroom:

Here's the time in Nancy's Study.

Here's the time in Nancy's Living Room.

Here's the (stove-based digital) time in Nancy's Kitchen.

And if I want:

Here's the time on Nancy's Wrist.

It's a matter of regaining what I had.
And adding other capacities I may invent new.

How the Story Ends—A Beginning

At the beginning there was an evening when I sat on the floor
near the cats' food dishes and water bowls
and said with a catch in my voice
knees drawn up and my arms around them:

This isn't the way the story was supposed to end!

But then almost immediately I thought

How do I know how the story is supposed to end?
Maybe this is exactly the way
it's supposed to end.

And then that night my task was to come up with a way
to live through this even if I can't live through it.

By morning I felt I had a good grasp on the task before me,
having been awake, thinking and writing deep in the night,

the cats and Bach ready to assist.
I needed this for appointments coming up—
scheduled in a row—bad news in each;
what was my plan?
I was ready, even if not yet having had
time or arms in which to grieve.

August 27

This Caring for My Body

This caring for my body takes so much time:
food preparation and eating six to nine times a day—
three small breakfasts
three small lunches
three small dinners.
Medications for my body; five or six supplements.
Cooling of my head three or four times a day
followed by speaking with thoracic ducts.*
Applying the castor oil liver pack.
Carefully bathing and then liberally anointing my skin with
    moisturizer.
And much more:
Walking at least once a day
Additional resting

* A technique advised in Nancy's physical therapy sessions, bringing awareness to a part of the body, in this case the lymphatic system

Talking with the OTS when it aches or signals it's confused
Noticing head tenderness and what precedes or calms it.

At least now, finally, this far after surgery,
I feel like I have the time for this care
instead of madly, haphazardly rushing,
doing nothing to satisfaction.

It takes time to bring ice packs to my room,
set them up within handtowels for cool temperature,
time their use, move them aside,
roll them up and return them to the freezer,
hang to air-dry the hand towels used.
No wonder there were evenings and days
I could do little of this for myself.

Some Anger

Finally clarity emerges:
I am being asked by others to provide pastoral care
about my own personal cancer—to help *them*
process their feelings about *my* personal life.

Of course I cannot do this.

Were I able to provide pastoral care,
I would not be on medical leave.
That ought to be enough said—
except that I don't think the request is understood
by askers as pastoral care.

It's just wishing to visit, to say hello,
as though the visitor brings only gifts and is actually offering care.

Not so!

On top of the sheer energy required, what arrogance is implied
even in asking?

Why is it mine to help another with the other's grief for *my* life?
Isn't it mine to choose with whom I enter such intimate
processing?
Where in the world is the ability to let me simply be separately me?

August 28

Letting Go of Medications

I suspect my body is going through minute but extensive
letting go of effects of an antinausea medication no longer
necessary.
It had dizziness as a potential side effect.
I am eager to delete as many medications as I can.

I suspect the recent extra soreness in my left sacroiliac joint
is a letting go from how it had figured out holding me to navigate
within increased
dizziness when the medication was added.
Coolness—like sheer food or a good long drink of cold water—
soothes the aggravation of that over-worked joint.

The trembling of my right hand is more noticeable with the draw-
    back, as well—
but I imagine my body will soon figure out how to modulate that,
    too.

Interesting are the unwindings, the de-compensatings,
the new pains telling me where the tension has been mitigated by
my clever, clever, ever-innovative and sweet body.

Appetite

I have read in a UMHS report that I have a low appetite. This is
stated without comment, as though completely true. It is not.
My appetite is *high*. I eat eight to ten times in each twenty-four
hours, meaning that I rise from bed, go to the kitchen, prepare
something simple or more complex depending on the time of
day and how ravenous I feel, and then clean up and return to
bed for rest. For a 3:00 AM breakfast this morning, I have eaten a
fresh zucchini baked in thin strips with olive oil and salt, a cup of
cooked oats with a sliced fresh plum, and a handful of almonds
that I soaked and roasted two days ago. Also a small glass of orange
juice—for the calcium and potassium. Plus morning supplements.
For morning medications between 6 and 7 AM, I'll need to eat
substantially again—as I did twice last evening after returning
from acupuncture: first rice with black beans and lime juice with
a bit of cheddar cheese and a whole, perfectly ripe tomato; then
warm pita dipped in olive oil; and a cup of freshly cooked oat bran
with some plain Greek yogurt and veggie juice. I'm overeating
pita bread at the moment, but more important is simply to get the

calories in and not stress about the perfection of them. Fresh and good-tasting are important, too; also some variety in veggies and fruit—which I'm managing. All in all, food is going well, and my weight is staying solidly above the target 100 pounds. Low appetite, indeed!

What I Find in Judaism

A lineage, a heritage, a history:
placing of persons within tradition and centuries;
complete liturgical addressing of spiritual and psychic needs;
a source compendium, so that one needn't constantly invent and
    draw together.
One *may* invent, but the main sources and needs for coverage are
    already
accessibly present.
All one must do is use them
(also true but seems less broadly so in Christian traditions).

And then of course three major foci:
God as Source, Creator, Author
Repair of our world
Personal agency and responsibility.

To which I begin to add a fourth:
God as Beloved
and concomitantly
Self as the Beloved of God.

I want to stand within a lineage and a tradition.
Not protest that we need stories
but draw out how here *are* the stories.
I don't want to invent but extend—
    See this food?
    It's already here.

Ice Trays

This simple following through of one thing and then another:
what a novel, peace-engendering endeavor.

This morning my first question was:
Do I have ice trays?—
because I need ice for the visit this afternoon of a couple
I am very much looking forward to seeing:
kind and loving folk who anguished
at my misfortune.
I want to greet them well:
calm house, cool drinks, peaceful exchange at the heart level
in which they dwell.

I sat on the kitchen floor and peered into the one cupboard where
such trays would be, if they indeed live with me.
Found not one but four!
Washed them, and also the few pots and dishes in the sink.
Washed the water filter pitcher as well, including finally removing
and scrubbing around the label
that had caught some mold.

Made sure the refrigerator can accommodate the trays, once filled.
Cooked breakfast: oat bran with lots of cold yogurt
and frozen raspberries on top, followed by medications and
    supplements.
Fed the cats—Eliza about six times; plus gave her ice-cold water,
    which she loves.
Dried hand towels from washing late yesterday;
transferred them to the too-small hall linen closet
plus resulting overflow to the upstairs Richmond dresser,
being careful to cover my head with my hands, when near the
    sloped roof.

So yes, I have ice trays,
and a house just about ready for a much-anticipated visit.
And a mind that's relatively uncluttered and peaceful.

August 31

How to Write a Card

1) Figure out if you are writing to another person or to your own
self.

If to your own self, then write simply to yourself and don't
send it to the person it's supposedly for.

Some clues that you're actually writing a card to your own self:

You are reluctant to write, and then finally force yourself to
write.

You practice your note, crossing out simple words and phrasing and inserting more elaborate ones. The message is then intellectual rather than flowing.

You say, "You must _____" and use words or phrases that indicate arduousness, tiredness, a (heroic) battle, military or game analogies. Question: Does the person you think you're writing to actually see the engagement in these terms?

Note: Trying to imagine how the other (card recipient) is feeling is a near-impossible task. You may or may not be able to discern this. Err on the side of respectful caution and don't presume feeling or stance. Instead, interrogate yourself about your assumptions: Where and how did you learn these? Are you suffering from any grief or regret in relation to people previously ill in your life? Then deal with this first. Don't just project your own stuff. All that will do is distance the other, when what you hope is to support increased closeness.

2) Don't make the recipient into a heroic figure who is doing the extraordinary. *You* may feel that way, but that's *your* stuff. If you make the other into someone heroic, you are actually separating him or her from your embrace—which is the last thing that is helpful.

3) Don't say, "I couldn't do what you're doing!" Really you couldn't? Why not? Because you're a wimp? Because you think you haven't the strength? Because you (mistakenly) think it means looking into the abyss and you're not ready? Well, work

on these! Don't just project "You are Other!" How the hell helpful is it to just separate?

4) Bottom line: Be present, be simple, write from the heart but beware untended heart-work of your own—which you've got to do first, so that you don't unintentionally cast the other aside and inflict the pain of separation.

5) If you can't kindly do something simple, just wait until you can. Take this as an opportunity to work on your own life and heart. It's better to send nothing than to send something hurtful. Don't presume you know the other's life.

6) Think of what you actually know of the other person—color choices, images, skills, likes, life-meaning. Find or make a particular card that reflect these—a direct kiss to the heart.

September

How I want just my old, own self—
as over the years I have learned to care for it:
simple foods, no medications, good exercise
and a certain agreement on rest.

September 4

Clothing as Art

I do love my clothing.

Yesterday afternoon I tried on my long, light-green Guatemala-woven dress with gathered waistband. I still love it; I can update it with layers for fall. Also the lavender gathered-waist long flowing dress, which will be rich under my deep blue roll-sleeve shirt and maybe the olive vest again. Plus the long purple and lavender tunic from my meditation manual GA workshop is still gorgeous with my green-blue rayon scarf. And the long lavender skirt works under the tunic, still, too. Possibly for next GA and another workshop.

I have carefully over the last four years added simple, solid-color items like shirts and long, svelte, good-quality sweaters and several long, simple skirts and colorful scarves, so that I now have a beautiful Sunday-morning professional wardrobe—and not the need to wear it.

The pleasure is how beautiful it all is; the sadness: Where do I wear it now? I will have to go out! Date, speak at events, take workshops. Dress in a fun way to shop for groceries in Davis and to go to physical therapy.

My body has been my canvas for years: This color . . . that. This line . . . that. I have loved being walking, breathing, simple, easily-changeable, and relatively inexpensive art. I did particularly well with Sunday mornings at UUAA, where robing is usually impossible. A few things I'll give away. Most I still want to keep to play in and be seen in, professionally and otherwise. It isn't, I learned yesterday, just what's short I need and want right now. It's *lean* and thin. Elegantly long is sometimes okay.

In all this, I think hourly of Nancy Kays, whose body and spirit are now under hospice care, and who is now sleeping her way into her next life. I am glad to have this peaceful image of her. I notice what my body can do that Nancy's no longer can, and I am sad for her and her family. She is leaving this life young. She did know that if the cancer returned, no treatment would be possible. Still. She would have turned sixty-two in mid-October.

September 7

Puzzle Pieces

Afterward, I notice a sequence of puzzle pieces.

I officiated at or hosted memorial services on four Saturdays in a row in April. On the first one, arriving at my office at church, I discovered that I did not have my bifocals with me. I checked my purse once, twice. No glasses. Went down the hallway to the staff bathroom. Discovered when I returned to my office that my door had closed on its own, locking me out. This meant that if I left the office area to find the building attendant to let me into my office, I might get locked out of the office area as well. I did go to find the building attendant, calling for him in several wings. He let me into my own office. I got my purse and headed for home, but before this explained to the brother of the man we were to memorialize

I'm sorry, but I forgot my glasses.
I've got to go home to get them.
I'll be back as soon as I can.

The service was to begin in thirty minutes.

I said nearly the same thing to the musicians, a hammer dulcimer player and guitarist who were setting up their instruments at the side of the sanctuary.

I drove home, found my glasses in their case on my bathroom counter and drove back to church—a lickety-split version of a trip that can take forty minutes.

The wife of the man who had died had still not arrived.

I spoke with the other brother, supervised where the ashes and large photo were placed on a low table near the chancel steps, located the speakers and reviewed with them when and by what route they would come forward. Finally one brother decided he should go pick up the absent wife. We delayed the start of the service until she appeared.

The service was shimmeringly beautiful.

Another Saturday was far more painful.

The service was for a man who had lived for a very long time with substantial emotional illness. It had been a challenge to find enough to say to fill the eulogy family members wanted but did not want to create themselves. Working thoughtfully, painstakingly, over many hours, I found qualities and daily events to celebrate, fitting readings; found ways to say how this life had been cherished by the person himself and family members. Which it had been.

And then—

Something happened to my car: a noise, a smell. I was out finally getting groceries. I called the auto repair shop to which I go for regular servicing, but it was just after 5 PM on a Friday and all the mechanics were on their way home. I called the number the shop owner suggested as back-up in a nearby town; those employees, also, were on their way home. I drove carefully home, called Enterprise to reserve a rental car for the following morning, and planned for the next day, when I would head south out of town to a small city I'd not traveled to before. Then I finished writing the service, emailed the whole of it to the family member who was my main contact, and let him know when I would be leaving in the morning. If any revisions were needed, I would need to be informed by an hour and a half before I left.

In the morning, I left a little before nine to pick up the rental car—my neighbors dropping me off on their way to their usual Saturday breakfast—but I couldn't leave directly from there because I had to return to my house to dress in my service clothing. I left at about 10 AM, wishing it were 9, for a service scheduled to begin at 11. I did not make it.

MapQuest had me go south and then west and then south and then west through the April countryside, yellow mustard plants and fruit trees blossoming.

I was mesmerized by the beauty.

I kept track of names of roads and distances between them. Only once did I miss a turn, and only for a short distance.

The hell started when I got to the funeral home. It was all the way at the end of a small town that took forever to drive through. I had pulled off to say I would be arriving shortly. It was now 10:45 AM. When I did arrive at the funeral home, I saw there were only a couple of cars in the lot. I parked in the shade, walked to the main door, and knocked. Twice. Loudly. No answer.

I went to the side door with my best "I'm officiating at this service" smile, knocked—loudly—and waited. No response.

I dug in my purse for my cell phone and called the family contact person.

I'm here. How do I get in?
  Where are you? Which door?
In the back parking lot. Near the black pickup. There are only a
  couple of vehicles.
  Wait. Let me come around and find you.
I waited. No one appeared.
  Where are you?

It turned out the funeral home had two locations. I was at the location not hosting that particular memorial service. The other location was some fifteen minutes away—back north and east and north and east. The family member was frantic. Icy.
  I asked for directions.

Just use your GPS.
  I don't have GPS.

Major hell.

Finally I get directions from someone in the office at the funeral home. Only she said *Go west* and *Go east*—concepts of no consequence to me when the Pacific Ocean is not near, as it never has been in south-central Michigan.

When I got to the funeral home, having parked in the small town and walked the last two blocks, the service had just ended, read aloud by a family member—not my tone but my words and plan. Another family member—portrayed by the first as also seriously challenged—turned out to be one of the nicest people present, inviting me to speak instead at graveside. I followed the group a half hour more into the countryside and did just that, at last finding a chance to speak some comfort and passion for this family. Then I returned to my car, retrieved the check sent to me earlier in the week, and gave it back to the family. Two weeks later, a partial check arrived in the mail with the note: *Well, you did write the service.*

I took refuge in this: It *had* been a kind and generous celebration of a challenge-to-celebrate life.

2 PM

The old tumor site is increasing again in tenderness and achiness. This concerns me, as I want so very much to avoid further surgery and I fear increased achiness could be about increased fluid and therefore a need to drain it away.

Sometimes there is a searing pain that goes down the side of my head or the inside of the old tumor site—as though a membrane were being ripped away or adhesive being adjusted or removed—perhaps as fluid causes need for room. A question for Lisa, perhaps: What is this?

Not the Kitchen

Other weird puzzle pieces, had I been alert enough to register them:

I had stopped cooking for myself, apart from simple breakfasts of oatmeal or toasted bread or simple eggs. This after forty straight years of meticulous attention to ongoing daily quality (an organic, basically Mediterranean diet of whole grains, legumes and beans, fresh vegetables and fruits, olive oil as the only fat, some dairy, nuts). I could no longer bear to stand and chop and steam vegetables, gather them into bell jars, cool them, transport them in small ice chests along with grains and protein to the staff refrigerator where I heated them in bowl-sized batches four to six times each workday. I started dividing my meals between Chipotle and the Whole Foods salad bar. I could have done much worse.

I ate out more in three months, March to early June, than in the forty previous years combined. All I wanted was to be full—not to have to pick out or purchase or plan or sauté or steam or stir-fry anything—just eat. A huge clue, had I seen. I felt silly getting into my car and leaving home in order to eat—I had a kitchen, for heaven's sake—but it was beyond me to enter it and bring life out of it.

Locks, Pots and Glasses

I also returned home a couple times to find I'd not locked the side door of the house. I would enter, find the contents of the house not stolen, sigh, and promise myself I'd be more careful on next leaving.

And I burned food or boiled pots dry repeatedly. I'd put something on the stove, think to myself I'd only be gone a moment to see what emails had arrived, and then fifteen minutes later, climb out of having forgotten I'd started to cook something. Even when I set timers for myself, I did this: forgot what I'd started. I feel exceedingly lucky I didn't set off a kitchen fire.

Plus, I forgot my glasses a number of times. Once I simply stayed at the office without them, interviewing a couple as best I could with my eyes unaided by anything made of tempered and curved glass—just my own eyeballs and brain. It was assuredly not my best interview.

Miracle Talk

This is so unfair! she says, eyes flashing,
meaning
unfair that I have cancer.

I speak back mildly:
I don't see it that way.

How do *you see it?*
She still sounds angry.

It happened. I shrug—
almost imperceptibly.
I don't meet her eyes.

Then softly I continue
If it had to happen,
I was in the best place in the country for it.
I live four and a half miles
from the medical center.
I didn't have to go anywhere else
or seek out any further care,
once the tumor was discovered.
They just kept me in neuro-ICU.

There is also the matter of where in the world I was born—
not in a hut in Somalia or Egypt—
and that I received a good mind and good schooling and
have parents who believe that making a contribution to the world
is a primary responsibility one owes for living at all.

Is this unfair? No.
Nor is it that as a young and stupid driver, sleepy one night,
I didn't—when at last my eyes inconveniently closed—drive over
        a cliff.

Fair. Unfair.
No one gets to be sixty years old—
even white, even here—without quite a lot of
good luck and a multitude of singing angels
and stopped time.

I cannot claim only the lucky
and give away the unlucky.

The woman would like me to say much more, but
I haven't the energy for full-fledged
theological interchange.
I have to walk home—a matter of some
fifteen minutes of one foot and then
the other and then
the first one again.
I do this pretty well, but still . . .
I am on medical leave.
Not working.
I am in a store;
a congregation member is thrilled to be waiting on me.
Explaining further would be working.

My brain feels suddenly tired.

Weeks later I hear from a different congregation member:
Some are saying

How unfair this tumor is!
Can't there be a miracle in which it un-happens?

I say

I think the miracle has already happened.

A fist-sized, aggressive tumor
was removed from the planning, organizing, time-keeping,
integrating portion of the only brain I have—and I not only

survived but survived well.
I have no deficits to speak of,
no medical problems
other than having cancer.

I think the miracle has already happened.

September 9

I wake in my bed, long sighs of sleep emerging. I had thought to do paperwork—documentation of my landlord's greed—but no matter. Clearly I have been doing what I most need—sleeping, rather than wrangling with unethical behavior. My long flannel-covered heating pad lies over me from throat to pelvis as I try to heat my way past the pulling my esophagus makes on everything internal—it having dramatically commented in disgust this morning about my doctor's intrusive questioning of need for a particular medication prescribed by my primary care physician, whose province it is to make such decisions. That I sleep—rest—comes first.

I wake unsure what day it is. Friday afternoon? Saturday? What time? My bedside light is on, and it might be the middle of the afternoon, or even the day next to the one on which I fell asleep. No matter. All I have planned is a small dinner party on Saturday afternoon. I am mostly ready. All I need do—if possible—is launder several white curtain pieces where the cats nudge to look outside. All I need do—if possible—is to wipe the windows where the cats' noses kiss the glass. I return to contemplation. I am wrenched to the middle of my back.

Sexist Doctor

Finally, I am fed up with a doctor whose behavior feels to me power-based, moralistic, sexist. Even his nurses are cowed and harsh for him in his place. I am ready at last to tear him limb from limb, or at the very least to file a complaint. Instead, I stand at the sink and eat melted cheddar cheese on toasted pita bread, with scoops of golden rice and olive bruschetta scooped on top. This after two cherry pie Lara bars.

This constant eating, I realize, is a side effect of the steroid. This eating in anger is simply eating in anger. Both are new to me; another lesson in what others' lives are like. But the doctor—his idiocy is old. I hate him, though I want none of my (now finite) energy given to hate. The steroid—unavoidable—is because of the swelling in my brain caused by surgery and radiation therapy. For now, I will eat, in part because the steroid induces appetite; in part because I've got to have sufficient bulk in my stomach that medications don't corrode it, as they did during the thick of my head injury-medication period. I'm not willing to sacrifice my gut again.

Coming back from the mall, where Sandy had driven me to buy bras, I had such ferocious intestinal cramping I wondered if I'd contracted intestinal flu. I hadn't. I was just finally experiencing the results of understandable disgust at the doctor's treatment of me.

September 13

3:55 PM

The concentration needed for being present to organizing my book is so intense it can feel like I am entering a trance. I have to be able to withstand great grief and just be present as my own witness.

Another step in understanding this business of being a witness: Others stand as my witnesses. I walk toward each one, and in the process become more able to function as my own witness. I stand as my own witness, someone else reads/sees that and becomes more *her* own witness. We are like a relay race, or a stand of trees as a safe house.

September 15

Heavy Treasure

The women who clerk in the thrift shop
try hard not to be elitish.
They constantly trip themselves up.
This is visible in their faces,
laced into their words.

They place their hands carefully on the glass jewelry showcase
angled obliquely between themselves and
those who are purchasing,

cough delicately,
refer to the sign hung over the window behind them:
What's on special today? Two *what* (pairs of jeans)
for *what*? ($5).
They are dressed nicely.
There are three of them, four:
more than necessary.

I think to myself:
They ought, as the clerks, wear only
what they have purchased at the shop that day—
not Ann Taylor Loft, not Eddie Bauer,
not Cold Water Creek, unless off the rack, right here—
good things donated by good women who have
survived to a life age in which they are downsizing homes and
        closets,
good women who donate many things never before worn.
A happy environmental exchange.

Today I have found a treasure from someone who knows
secrets from centuries under stars:
a dark-glazed, intricately carved bowl and eggs,
something at once primordial and not-yet.
It is so earth-like and heavy I cannot carry it home all at once
because in addition to the bowl itself,
the four intricately carved eggs lie snuggled into each other,
each one also heavy with earth and patient, lined design.
I must make two trips. I explain this to the cashier,
who squints at the tax table.

When I return, she says

Oh, your bag! and

proudly sets in front of me the one she had put aside for my
    return:
the eggs wrapped in plain paper.

Neiman Marcus!—she continues—grandly naming the bag
    they lie in,
as though this will be special to me.
It isn't.
As though I want to be shopping elsewhere.
I don't.
As though because I am walking rather than driving
something is wrong.
The truth is my own legs have done this: allowed me to walk.
I am joyous.

I smile briefly, take the silver bag, walk to the door.

I want to be with people who know how to carve from stars—
people like the someone who made my new dark bowl
and its intricate, puzzling eggs out of her own heart.
I was lucky enough to be in the right place at the right time to
    receive it, after,
and to value as perfect the two small chipped places on the bowl's
    edge.
Quick enough immediately to say *yes* and hug the bowl to my own
    heart.

September 16

Concerto for MRI

Here's another patient support idea,
this one especially for children and youth:
develop a collaboration between the UM Department of Music,
    Dance, and Theater
and the Radiology Department;
find someone who can write a score for a common MRI sequence.
Rely for this writing on:
music students who happen to receive an MRI,
musically-gifted others (students, staff) who receive an MRI,
or
let it be a music project unrelated to actual MRI experience.

Teach the score to children and youth prior to their receiving an
    MRI.
Provide hand instruments for mimicking the sounds they will
    hear;
also the silent spaces.

Periodically, play an entire concert of MRI sounds as a
    collaboration between Music and Radiology.
Invite the entire UM community, perhaps a lunch concert.
Paint the score on the walls of the MRI room.
Turn MRI into the music it is.

That is, with children and youth and others who want to
    participate,

enter a three-part intervention:
This is what will happen (sounds of the MRI)
This is it—happening (the MRI itself)
This is the response, after (debriefing: What did happen? Tell it.
    Draw or paint it. Sing it. Rattle or clap it.)

Goals: preparation, ability to contribute to participating well, integration—all of these are about mastery and increased sense of personal agency, ability to affect outcome in a positive direction.

September 19

Turns Out

Turns out that steep desire
and acres of hard work
may not be enough.
I could still die from this tumor
sooner rather than later.
It may be out of hand,
per Friday's MRI.

My heart aches.

For the first time, I thought—
seeing the spongy area around
the old tumor site—
Wait a minute!
I've been abandoned!
Where's God?

Also the tiniest recognition that
one day I may feel relief
not to keep trying so hard.
This is a huge effort I put out daily, hourly, minute by minute—
to believe I can undo an aggressive tumor.

I heard myself ask, seeing that vulnerable sponginess,
What do I do now?
Lean even more on God?

So okay. I lean on God more.
But where is the fairness here?
For the first time, I am questioning that;
I hear it in my voice, in what comes from my mouth:
the protest that I have been such
a good patient, as though being that undoes the cancer;
the protest that I have so much in place
to help me beat the cancer;
the implicit underlying assertion that
surely I deserve better.

There! I've landed at last on Unfair!
Yes, damned unfair, in many, many ways.
Utterly unfair!
I was willing to go with usual fairness.
But sheesh!
I do think my circumstances are unusual
and I deserve a break toward fairness.

September 23

Entering Writing

The place I enter for writing is so deep
it can take me days to get there—
ready, backpack organized.
It's partly like entering a cave, stalactites
and stalagmites delicately standing guard.
Partly like diving beneath waves,
breath held against water and fish.
Partly like entering under any knowing at all,
a new babe, having forgotten

Everything.

Always an entering into mystery:
knowing nothing
in order to know fully.

So here I am on a Friday afternoon,
lying down with cats and many pillows, hungry,
slowly entering.

Continuing New Rules About Food

For two years,
on the advice of a doctor whose judgment about food and eating
I respect, I have been avoiding eating

more than two to three pieces of fruit a day,
as she believes more is too much sugar for me.

Now I say:
The hell with this.
Eat as much fruit as I want.
Eat it like a vegetable:
something that offers bulk
and fairly thin calories.
Eat lots of raw veggies also—
particularly sweet, raw carrots
and juicy local tomatoes.

Just eat nutritiously, I say now.
Just nutritiously.
Mostly I do.

But it's got to be simple.
And not all my own cooking.
Apart from soup when I could not chew,
I've asked not a single meal from the congregation.
Time to start: vegetarian or fish—
two times a week; no added sugar; no desserts.

Walgreens, Revisited

Walgreens mail-order pharmacy gets a chance to redeem itself
for the second home chemotherapy regimen.
I need chemotherapy five nights of each twenty-eight,

ideally beginning on a Monday for ease of tracking weeks,
but in any case as soon as the drug arrives—
which it turns out can be today—Tuesday—
by 3:00 PM.
FedEx will do the honors.

I am resting at 3:00 PM.

At 3:30 PM when I rise to forage in the kitchen,
there's a knock at the side door.
I open the door,
find looking up at me the black-and-white combed head
and glasses and eager eyes of a dark-skinned woman who says,
pointing at the For Sale sign on the front lawn

I called your realtor
to ask about your situation.
He told me about . . . (she hesitates) *. . . your illness.*

    Damn! I think.

What have they said to each other?
What remains private?

What I want to know she continues,
is whether you have someone to help you.

I gather she means when the sale closes and I must move.

    Yessss I say, the *s* lingering more than I'd intended.

You do?

    Yessss I say again, the *s* again lingering interestingly.

I realize she is offering: her own self.
What I ought to do is grab her and hug her.

I am not sure who she is:
FedEx driver, mail carrier who saw the box
and thought to help.

She steps carefully down the unrailed concrete steps
and then carefully back,
hands me the big box that holds within itself
one small capsule of Temodar,
which will cover my dosage for the five nights.

> *Thank you* I say to her.
> *My deepest thanks.*

We catch eyes.
She smiles warmly.
I close the side door.

I set the box on the living room table.
I am safe: Chemotherapy begins again tonight—
after information called in from Dr. J's office;
after my own half hour on the phone
further nailing down what's needed
and giving assent to payment.
The procedure takes several days of telephone tag.

I look for the woman in the days after,
wanting to give a larger thanks.

I would not have been surprised
for surely she has condensed the pieces of information:
lots and lots of—a deluge of—cards;
lots and lots of mailings from the U of M hospital system;
my car that stays in one position only.
My postal carrier surely has figured it out:
I am seriously ill, and on top of that, must soon move.

How the universe conspires to bless!

September 24

Ankles at Last

Yesterday morning, after two weeks lost,
my ankles reappeared—both left and right,
both sides of each.

I had worried over them!
I dressed them in tight crew socks and knee socks
to quell their swelling.
I bought them expensive compression stockings.
They did not care!
They continued to wobble and tell false stories
to my feet, my knees, my head, my balance.

I think it was Lisa's work that restored them;
Stephanie's* also:

*Nancy's acupuncturist

both worked on drainage blocked.

Lisa says Eliza is functioning as a gargoyle—
that which functions (so says *Wikipedia*) to ward off evil.
Now I call Eliza my gargoyle
and tell her to please be just that:
I do need someone, something, siphoning off evil
while I deal with the rest.
Her piercing meowing makes more sense, then:
part of an alarm system.

I need to work on compassion for a couple people.

September 25

Reluctant No

At dinner
at a small Middle Eastern restaurant
to which I have carefully walked at dusk,
pen in hand over a small tablet,
I discover someone
with whom I do not care to
engage further in establishing
relationship.

No

I decide.

Not worth it.

As accompaniment to rice
I have discovered a relationship
in which I will engage with pleasure.
But not this one.
My decision—which comes not thought but simply felt—
depletes and saddens me. My shoulders hunch.
I also feel relieved and clear:
This one is not worth my effort.

A good illness can do this:
highlight the necessary and real.

6:50 PM

Constructing the book may have some similarities to creating a
worship service, in the interweaving and concentration needed.
I might protect a three-day writing and incubation period each
week, Thursday through Saturday, Friday through Sunday.
That level of immersion may be needed for seeing through the
remembering and the entering to write. It makes sense to me that
I need that level of setting aside uninterrupted, depth-of-thinking
time.

Shorthand before Surgery

Before surgery I decide I need a shorthand list
to keep in mind as I am anesthetized:

something easily memorable to call on.
Something I can tell the surgeon if there is a chance.

I bring hymns to mind:

Comfort Me, comfort me, comfort me, oh, my soul . . .

*I've Got Peace like a River, I've got peace like a river, I've got peace
like a river in my soul . . .*

*Come and Go With Me to that land, come and go with me to that
land, come and go with me to that land where I'm bound . . .*

But what I decide on, I draw from a list I think through
about how I *feel* about the surgery and its team.
It's heavily skewed toward trust.
My surgeon has told me: This is his favorite thing to do in the
    world:
just this kind of surgery. How lucky for me is that?
He promised also that he will stay until I am out of any danger,
though he has a conference coming up on the weekend.

I trust the surgical team itself—which I have been told is the top
such team in the country.

I trust that the whole of what happens will be held in love—the
surgeon, the team, me—by colleagues and congregation members
locally and across the country where I have served.

I trust that all will be well.

Then I condense these three points enough to hold:
All will be held in love.
I trust the surgeon and the team.
I am ready!

The *Ready!* part still brings tears to my eyes.
Of course I wasn't ready—
just desperate to live.
Surgery was the identified way through.

I tucked my meditation manual* into the sheet near my left
shoulder—
or Cathy put it there, where I found it, waking.

Mark** walked by and said
Are you scared?
Your eyes look kind of scared.
It's okay to be scared.

And then he sat down somewhere to my right
and was quiet.

I understood that before surgery,
before I was completely out,
my head would be marked for exact location of entry.
I was not awake for that.

Instructions in Joy (Skinner House Books, 2002)
**a colleague from the Ann Arbor congregation

Pointing at me, Cathy said to the (cute) anesthesiologists with the
    Australian accents
She's a published poet. She can put you in a poem.

To me she winked and said softly
I think they'd like that.

I remember sky-blue scrubs worn by the anesthesiologists.
Also their wide, white-toothed smiles.
They were going to get to try something different,
since my temporomandibular joints are damaged
and don't open very far.

Apart from dreamscapes and three major insights, I remember
    little else until several hours later
when I thought Krista Tippett should be interviewing me.

I repeated to myself the points I wanted to remember—
that I remember still: mostly trust; also a lot of love.

The Beginning of Being Held in Love

The idea that the surgery—all of it—would be held in love
by colleagues and congregation members:

How did that begin in me?

It did not feel new,
did not feel thought out,
did not feel like it had any beginning point
but was just present in me, waiting—

and now its time had come.

It came to me as certainty
of the way things inherently *are*:
an essential fact of living:
love is the beginning, the holding,
the essence.
Of course the surgery would be held within it.

September 26

New Walking

I notice, walking home from dinner
on Saturday evening, how much stronger
my walking is than three-four-five weeks ago.
I pass the eight blocks south and five blocks west from my house
to the café (my first time there) with much less thought for how
each leg and foot do their work;
stand without uncertainty, waiting for the light to turn at long last.
I do not worry that I look to drivers fragile, tentative, ill:
someone who should not be out walking alone.
I set off confidently over the pedestrian walk when traffic finally
    halts.

I'd forgotten how arduous those first long trips over twelve-
    thirteen blocks
and then home—walked not because I wanted to walk that far,
    total, but because

that was the unchangeable distance; my legs, the method.
Once started, I could not simply stop and sit.
I walk a bit more now like Baryshnikov by fields in *Witness*—a bit
of lilt; apparent joy.
I'm not bounding, not graced with Baryshnikov's height and
strength.
My right leg still could use some confidence in length of stride,
but I do have more symmetry and choice.

I have more fun when I'm walking for pleasure than *must*.

Return to Self

Rapidly today, my body is becoming more my own.
My ankles are back,
my weight is quickly becoming more usual,
my walk feels more its old pace and gait.
I continue to feel that if I could just
have my body as its own self
without extra medication—
much would be well.
I would be more sure-footed,
not crave sweets and oils and all things heavy,
more my usual weight,
have my usual sense of head
without light-headedness and a buzzed and somewhat dizzy sense.

It is a joy to notice what changes as I lessen even one medication.
I couldn't, of course, have noted the intricacy of changes in reverse
    order,
when I went straight from exhaustion to surgery to medicated self
to suddenly home without help.
Much too much jumbling of factors, initially.
Now, carefully, I see one tiny layer at a time.

How I want just my old, own self—
as over the years I have learned to care for it:
simple foods, no medications, good exercise
and a certain agreement on rest.

September 27

Eating the Rainbow

Yesterday, standing in Whole Foods,
I decide

Yes, this is a Whole Paycheck day.

Locals tease Whole Foods for its prices
by calling it Whole Paycheck.
I decide to buy the rainbow, living-color violet-to-red:
dark purple organic cabbage,
California black mission figs.
(I see several of the missions in my mind's eye
as I scoop up figs.)

California organic Medjool dates,
Thompson seedless raisins,
red bell peppers,
orange bell peppers,
yellow bell peppers,
two bunches of kale,
a dozen slender, foot-long carrots,
pea pods,
orange organic yams and sweet potatoes,
white cauliflower trimmed of its greenery,
green beans,
black plums,
nectarines with skin of orange-yellow-red.
Simpler than thinking through properties of each—
just eat the rainbow.
Diana, in the morning, suggested this as shorthand
for eating supportive nutrients well: Just eat the rainbow.
It was a throw-away sentence. I remember now and grab it.

So I fill the basket: vegetables, fruit, two big fillets of salmon—
    which
I suddenly realize are less expensive if I buy hunks
and then bake and eat from them over several days
rather than buy separate fillets.
My body craves what seems to it perfect protein.

Home, later, I sink my teeth into a date,
eat three of the black mission figs,
bend my head gently to make space through the refrigerator:
Where will these medicines go?

I am eager for their clarity, their transferring earth and sky and
    stars to me,
eager for the knitting of their elements and my life.

The salmon is succulent with lime juice and a porridge of cooled
    golden rice and fresh tomato.

I eat mostly standing up, taking in the day's news.

September 28

7 AM

It keeps feeling to me like it must be Sunday—which I take as
not about my mixing and forgetting the sequence of days but the
depth with which I am entering into the pieces of the book: I am
preparing worship, so surely, soon, it is time to offer it.

In the night I was awake for a time as often I am—sorting,
organizing, eating, doing.

I took off the newish light-green sham I'd put over the piano
bench, looked up where in my suitcases I'd stored the light-green
machine-embroidered small sham, efficiently got it out, placed
it; returned suitcases and more to their places in the attic closet;
put away various pieces of paper, organized a sequence of poems
by month in folders; realized the embroidered bag for quilted bed
things for my Mount Vernon–house bedroom might be something
Hope would like to lie on, so brought it to the bedroom; ate a

couple of times; changed the sheets. Looks like my ankles may be a little puffy again; and my weight has not fallen much. Oh, well.

I am loving the mixing and matching of various sheets and spreads I can do, collected patterns over the years, few if any bought new.

Eliza is much calmer now that I am calmer. Much less guarding me and keeping piercing eyes on my every move. Every time I go into the bedroom (cats sleeping at the foot of the bed) I say:

I love you two. Love you guys.

Plus I saw where I would like to hang—to hold in my eyes from my bed—the framed cards of turtle and horse (which I note now is headed toward the left, toward Davis).

7:55 PM

Nancy Kays died last evening, 8:30 PM Davis time, meaning 5:30 PM Ann Arbor time. I wish I could remember back to what I was doing just then—likely eating dinner or cleaning up. No wait, my math was off three hours in the wrong direction. I was still up, happily editing on the computer, working on the book until, I think, 11:30 PM. Might have been when I made some oat bran and it was very thick and I realized I'd eaten too much pear with it and should have cut up only half a pear instead of the full pear.

I wonder if Nancy had been ambivalent about reaching her birthday and that's why it took so long for her at the end. Maybe she wanted to make it to sixty-two, but she knew she was just too sick. It is good, actually, to know she is gone. I have been anxious, waiting to hear. I hoped she wasn't emotionally fleeing, although surely at some level she was, or the end would have been sooner.

The memorial service is the afternoon of October 23—the same day I hope to offer a good-bye service in Ann Arbor, followed by a moving van and leaving here.

9 PM

Two things have helped with the beauty factor—the second totally unexpected:

My upper eyelashes remained, and they are fringing nicely with mascara.

I have "steroid bubble face"—meaning some roundedness of cheeks, which make me look happy and a bit younger.

Also I'm wearing all of the happiest colors and fun clothes that I have—all of my most favorite things, including my gloriously colored coats for various weather variations, so that I look very nice whenever I leave the house, including to get the mail from the box across the street. The bright and coordinated Nancy-colors draw peoples' eyes to me and draw delighted smiles, especially the lime-green hat. The color and its exquisite wide-brimmed design make it gorgeous—and me, important to meet eye-to-eye. Not bad for a sixty-one-year-old woman with cancer and little hair.

Sue says she can accept when contemporaries die but *Not you young ones.* Meaning Nancy Kays. Meaning my own illness—which—if ever—I intend to die from much later than now, not young, not at all soon. I still hope and intend to outlive this cancer.

I tell her I think Nancy got stuck at the end. I do not say I think she came and pulled at me last night for something she needed. I do not tell her I told Nancy: *Take what you need and then please go*—which can sound harsh; but I mean it only as closure, so that she can rest, and the two worlds can rest: spirit and the one we think is actual.

Do take what you need; but then just step into whatever—which I suspect you may have found too many options for, and settled on none.

I suspect Nancy has inadvertently taught more than she intended, dying: the danger of too many options.

I think for me this will not be a problem. When it is time, God will collect me; also Emily Dickinson will come along and I will step out and it will be sad but fine.

I do not imagine that I will be afraid. Only curious—eager, even—to know what is next, which I imagine I will quietly breathe my way into, safely. I expect Jesus will be right there in vast light with open arms; also Madeleine and Great-Grandma and Patty L and Nancy and Great-Aunt Dorothy and anyone major whom I have loved, including George and perhaps by then Bob. I expect a peaceful passing, not violent, as it might be in another land. Sad and too soon, but not violent. At my own pace.

September 30

Good-Bye to Mr. Medieval

For Mr. Medieval: a ritual for saying good-bye to the blue-mesh
    mask he was:
I made sure I had lots of pictures, first.

You did your work.
Thank you for holding my head steady.
You were often really painful.
I am glad you are done.
Good-bye.

Said thirty times, one for each radiation session, and I stood in a
different spot for each thank-you, throughout the house—in the
attic; on the steps to the attic and basement; in the kitchen, living
room, bedroom, basement. Then into a bag and into the outside
garbage can.

I lighted a chalice in the living room, but did not want to leave it
unattended, so shortly blew it out.

October

You walked ahead of me—
a path we had not imagined
when we laughed and pointed out ducks to each other in
the causeway,
Sacramento in the distance.
How I shall miss you!

October 2

11:10 AM

It feels like feeding myself remains just about a full-time task. Today so far: four times I've eaten; probably three to four times to go.

I have been concerned I might miss an infusion because of skirting a virus this last week; now I'm hovering on a cold I can feel still wanting to begin. I think I need several days staying as close as possible to bed; also Lisa's help and Stephanie's and more homeopathic remedies. But I think I can avoid all-out coughing, sneezing, cold-flu hell, as others might not. It could have been terrifically bad, say my chest and nose. For a full week, my GI system has already paid the price. Yikes! I'm the one people like me should stay away from!

October 4

A Rant Against *Passing*
(After Nancy K)

This is a rant against—I admit it right at the beginning—
the use of the word *pass* to mean *die*.

I HATE *pass* used as a euphemism for dying.
Pass *what*? Pass *how*?
Pass away from *what*? *Life*?

That sounds like coming up against the end of knowing something
and then just giving up; not equal to; fleeing.

What the hell? There was all of life before that, when one was not
faint of heart.
One does not *pass away;* one *dies,* for heaven's sake.

And then to leave off even the *away* and say only that one *passed*
is the height of theological, intellectual, verbal sloppiness.
Passed the exit exam?
Passed the pearled gates?
Passed into the mists of time?
Say it, for heaven's sake: passed *what?*

Why the hell don't people just die?

Try it:
_____ died.
_____ died last night.
At _____ this morning, _____ died, became other
substance, breathed his/her last breath, entered another realm that
we do not name so easily as this daily, breathing, wrestling-with-
traffic-and-dinner-preparation one. _____ ceased living
as we usually think of living and became loved memory, bone and
mineral only, *gone* from the way known for sixty-one years.

But *passed?* Give me a break! Was there a commencement speech?
Checking of all answers for a 95 percent? How many times had
he/she tried before to gain passage? What percentage of the class
passed? Who needs to study more? Who will assist?

Use the word with at least some wit and intelligence.

Where the hell is *away?* No matter. The whole business sounds fainthearted, when it is among the most rigorous one will ever engage in. It's hard to let go of life. The body is inherently devoted to living. It's set for that, and outrageously keeps trying to make living work.

Three Things After Surgery, Revisited

I awake from surgery knowing three things:

> The entirety of the surgery was held in love—I was held; the surgery team was held. That is the beginning point.

> The ending point, I realize with equal certainty, is similar: The only question large enough for us is how to give enough thanks for our lives. Nothing else is worth our wrestling, just how to give enough thanks for this improbable, magnificent thing we are gifted with: living, breathing awareness of what it means to be awake, alert, seeing, feeling.

> And the third: the most personal of the three—the question for God: Am I doing enough in my life to follow a spiritual path?

> *Yes* the answer comes. *Yes. Everything you do counts and is layered up—and together, yes, all of it is enough. You are on the right track. You are doing enough. It all matters.*

My eyes overflow in response, in relief.

I feel—*claimed*.

Oh! I think.
I know how to do this surgery/cancer thing.

It's mostly about being present to the Sacred—which for some reason right now seems related to the curtain between my bed and one next to me. The simple colors are imprinted on my mind: orange, a blue that is a cross between baby-blue and sky-blue, brown, silver-gray. There are writing and symbols, both, on the curtain. A quite generic curtain, ubiquitous throughout the hospital, simple white mesh for a foot or more at the top. Not a silence filter; a divider of imaginary space.

The reason for the surgery is terrible, but the answers I have wrested from it, the fullness of life. I know this, waking, and settle into both note taking and sleep. I would miss none of this, for anything.

It's mostly about being present to the Sacred.
I can do that.
I do do that.

I have been home a number of weeks. Walking outside in early evening, Gary asks what the experience of the tumor and its follow-up have been like for me. I asked him to visit so that we could walk together. Such a big deal—walking at will after a fist-sized part of my brain is gone. The sky is both gorgeous and calm.

I look to my right, where Gary is walking, choke a bit because of the pureness of my words; say the first thing that comes:

It's the most important thing that's ever happened to me.

Ministers don't cry at questions congregation members ask them, of course. They also don't, directly in the moment, work on their own lives with congregation members. So I don't.

Then I add, still a little uneven of voice:

I wouldn't miss it for anything.

We walk a mile or two, gleeful; then sit some moments in my kitchen—on the small caned fruitwood chairs from my grandparents' kitchen. Both Gary and I are short; chairs a century old fit us well. My grandparents' kitchen featured pea green. Mine is off-white with highlights of brilliant Scandinavian blue in linen I brought back as an exchange student.

Yes, there is much goodness in all that has come my way.

October 9

New Status

I notice—on the last day
I am employed by Ann Arbor as associate minister—
as my sweet psyche figures out what it needs to do:

1.   write what I will say in a final "gratitude event" with the congregation;
2.   write a poem for a friend who has died too soon;
3.   in preparation for moving, clean out files not used in the three years since my last move.

The file work goes quickly: UU history, early church,
New Testament, mystical Judaism, polity,
new member welcome, board support ideas,
leadership styles and congregational leadership,
Sufism—except then I see it's about Rumi
and I grab it back.

What is clear to me is how much I am now the writer:
What matters is to keep my writings.
I can reinvent the rest, look it up online,
find six current books more detailed and accurate than the notes
I painstakingly took years ago.

What I can't find in someone else's book is my own writing,
which emerges out of *me*.
I am no longer a congregation's minister:
I am a source, an inventor, a writer.
I want no files that do not begin with my own knowing.

Worthy learning out of a single weekend I had anticipated
mostly as heartbreak.

I notice my joy in writing,
notice I am good at writing.

After Nancy Kays

In the photograph you are smiling into the camera
in your usual direct way, no blinking—
your hair that straight, silky blunt-edged cut
just above your shoulders, pulled back from your forehead
by a simple band.
Your eyeglasses are simple, as well:
direct horizontal oblongs; your smile, wide.
It is a typical Nancy-look:
open, happy, present. There is sunlight over all,
but you do not squint.
There is clearly texture in the top
you are wearing. The beginning of a necklace
is visible.

Oh, my dear!
You are gone too soon!
Twenty years too soon.
Thirty years too soon.
Sue—eighty and living now via wheelchair assistance—
says

I can handle it when my contemporaries die.
Not you young ones.
She means you. Potentially, me.
We weep across more than two thousand miles,
your was-life, your still-life, between us.

I asked you recently

What do I do now? What do you know about this next
year I have?

Because you—like an older sister
before me—just completed a year of treatment for cancer.
Now I've had surgery and initial chemotherapy and radiation and
have been assigned also a year of additional follow-up.
I wanted to know: Is there anything in particular you suggest I do
during this year, to support my recovery?

You told me your own daily news.

I don't plan anything now.

    Oh.

I hadn't known, so bluntly.

I just live day to day.

    Oh. A stomach blow.

Matter-of-factly—no self-pity—
you say

I will live with uncertainty always.

You are to receive three-month CT scan results the next day.

Then about my own work you say

Let things happen!
This may be your strongest time—
between surgery and more treatment—

which you had some deep clues about,
given your own rigorous, just-completed year.

I listened—and snuggled down into
the dailiness of embrace
of just what is present.

Once you start more treatment
you may not feel so good as now.

I took you at your word, listened carefully,
took advantage of as much strength and of as many
good-feeling intervals as possible.

You walked ahead of me—
a path we had not imagined
when we laughed and pointed out ducks to each other in the
    causeway,
Sacramento in the distance.

How I shall miss you!

October 23

Farewell Words to the Congregation in Ann Arbor

Good morning!
I have missed you!
It is good to be here with you!

What's up?

What am I setting off to do?
What's happened?

There has already been a miracle here.
There has already been a gathering of blessings.

I want to offer you two of my poems, name some blessings with you, and tell you where I am going and why. I want to assure you that no matter where I go, you will go with me in my heart, just as I will stay here with you in yours.

What happened to us? I suddenly—or not so suddenly, depending on your viewpoint—was visited by a brain tumor.

I landed late on Sunday evening, June 5, in the emergency room of the University of Michigan hospital system; I went home on June 14 minus a fist-sized tumor. I have been on extended medical leave since, after initial chemo and radiation therapy. I am now two months into a six- to twelve-month follow-up chemotherapy program. And I am leaving Ann Arbor on November 2 to complete that treatment in Davis, California, given that treatment is utterly portable—and so am I.

What's Davis got that Ann Arbor doesn't?

To be blunt: a Mediterranean climate. A farmers' market open year-round. One can walk outside safely in any season, any month of the year. Spring begins by mid-February.

One "goes to the snow"—a phrase from my childhood: One travels deliberately to find snow; one dresses for it when one gets there.

Davis has friends and old neighbors. It has the Unitarian Universalist congregation out of which I entered seminary. It has a view across farmland to the foothills of the Pacific Coast to the west and to the tops of the Sierras to the East. It has evening and morning breezes from the San Francisco Bay delta, flights of migrating ducks, and a small cottage I bought nearly twenty-five years ago—to which I can now return. It is my home.

And what doesn't it have?
It doesn't have *this* congregation.
It doesn't have *you.*

I am receiving excellent, top-notch, kind care here in Ann Arbor. Absent my ties to Davis, there would be no reason to leave. I could stay exactly here and continue treatment.

But my choice is to go where I think I have the best chance of getting well—which has to do with deep, deep, deep, deep levels of support, brought into being over a lifetime. Davis is that place for me. There's a part of me that feels like I've known it even in another lifetime—perhaps as an indigenous child living in the Great Central Valley. There is a sweep of land off of Interstate 80 that speaks up about that to me: *You lived here, once,* it says, every time I go past it.

It tears my heart to leave you and the ministry I have found in this congregation.

Ministers and congregations part regularly. The congregation is the permanent thing; the minister is not. We—you and I—are part of an ongoing whole in this way. Ministers leave due to illness or family circumstance—though generally not an illness so dramatic as a brain tumor. Let's admit it: I'm the last person to pull the drama card, right? Not your drama queen. That's a clue about how terribly real this is. It tears my heart to leave you; what mends my heart is the thought and the reality of North Central California, which is land my bones know, land my cells know, land my feet and heart know.

At the beginning of this tumor odyssey, a voice protested to me one sad evening
This isn't the way the story was supposed to end.

Almost immediately another voice said *But how do I know how the story was supposed to end? Maybe this is exactly the way it was supposed to end.*

Because, you know, every single thing that happens can be made useful, *is* useful.

I want to hold up for us some of the blessings that have already happened:

I learned—very quickly—how much you care about me, for me.

I learned—very quickly—that although I have often *felt* invisible in my role, I have not been invisible. You have seen me clearly, with eyes of great love, which comes through in the cards and notes you have sent. I learned something more about the deepest grief being nearly inarticulate; and therefore the articulateness of the lack of words. We were stunned, together: How could I have a tumor? Such a big one?

And look at all I can still do: How can *this* be?

I would not have chosen at this point in my ministry with you to hand on my ministry, all of it, without question of what will become of it; but that has been necessary, and I have done that; and you have stepped in to say *Yes, we will hold it. We* are *holding it. All will be fine and well.*

All *is* fine and well. I trust the program will thrive, even as I miss it, and miss you.

So we make an exchange: my health; your continuing, growing ministry with each other and our children and youth.

This can be a flagship program for our denomination. It can lead other denominations' in-depth layering of integration of children and youth and adults in the mixture of living a faith tradition as part of both worship and repair of our world. There is no finer endeavor than this that you are already engaged in. Perhaps this is exactly the way the story was supposed to end.

My love stays with you.

November

Oh, this was *real*.

In the first days of November, after she had packed up her house and wrestled her reluctant cats into carriers, Nancy moved from Ann Arbor to Davis, California. AMTRAK would not accept the cats, even in carriers, even after friends pleaded special circumstances, so a colleague drove her across two-thirds of the country.

A move would have been necessary in any case, since Nancy's landlord in Ann Arbor had determined to sell the house she was living in. Friends and congregation members in Ann Arbor were there to help with the packing. As soon as it became apparent that Nancy would have to leave her work in Ann Arbor, she made a decision to return to Davis, where she owned a condo and which her heart knew as home.

In the move, or after the move, any writings done during this period were lost. A February entry ("November") notes her loss of the folder for November, but what is most strange is that there were also no poems with November dates on her hard drive or sent to me in emails. I can find a few email messages from Nancy in this month— she met her new doctor, etc.—but no writings.

I visited Nancy in Davis in the last weeks of her life, and in addition to sitting by her bed, talking with her, and listening to her, I spent some time in her home office, looking through files. I was Nancy's health care proxy at that time; she had told me I was also her financial power of attorney, but nobody could find papers authorizing that, and I was hoping to find them so I could smooth the way for her parents and others who would be handling her affairs. I did not find the papers I was looking for, but I did find a folder including raw writings from October, November, and December. This was Nancy's process: She wrote every day on yellow pads, and some of those writings found their way into her computer in more polished form.

I surmise that in November, a month of upheaval, of packing and unpacking, she did not enter her writings into her computer. November was a hard month for Nancy; she had put so much hope into this move to Davis, yet it had been years since she lived there, and some of the relationships she'd been counting on did not re-materialize. Among the November-dated writings I discovered in her files, there are only a few that seemed intended for inclusion here.—MMG

November 13

I'm feeling filled up with pain right now—lost money, lost job, lost a thousand people, lost Sandy, had to deal with hotel mistakes,* had to deal with professional expenses, unpacking, parents; the potential shortness of my life.

Reentering the Church I Have Known

It is not necessary to meet everyone
I knew on the first Sunday. They are not
all present, those I knew—luckily; my
energy will hold out better over several
Sundays than just one.

Hello! I can say.

Hello! Hello!

* One of the motels where Nancy and a colleague stayed during their drive across the country to Davis had double-charged her credit card. —MMG

I'm Nancy Shaffer.
Yes, I've moved back to Davis.

Not unlike others who return
to this fairy tale of a town.

I had felt cautious
about my appearance—
especially my poor head
and its sparse and oddly patterned
hair, with clumps and sections gone.
(It might look worse, shaved off close.
I've kept what length I could.)
I'm sure some people looked at me
and looked away, not seeing *Nancy!*—
and some looked at length,
and then saw, *Nancy!* (I saw _____'s
face change).

November 18

I am nearly immobilized by how much there is to do to make a
home of these boxes of books and miscellaneous possessions. I
could easily just stop doing *anything*—just lie down and give up
and sleep. . . .

So much to do, and I the only one to do it.

How to stay focused on gentleness to myself,
gentleness and nurturing—

beauty
order
nutrition
help with putting away and getting organized
financial relief

November 19

I have not yet walked outside in the Greenbelt—
somehow a sadness too much to bear, should I go
there, perhaps because Nancy Kays walks no longer;
perhaps because reminiscent of the arduousness
of learning to walk again in Ann Arbor
after the surgery . . . .

November 20

There's very little I want to do—
lie in bed and read;
eat.
I'd like to have the condo totally
put away from the move, would like to have
Internet access, would like to have many
paperwork things tended to and over—
but I want to *do* none of it.

November 23

My voice returns me to myself
unexpectedly.
I think I am saying something
ordinary
but my voice breaks
and I am hauled into the open:

I care a great deal.

I try to proceed as though
it hadn't broken—I gulp;
begin a new sentence—
but I think the other knows:

Oh, this was *real.*

November 30

Sunlight splashes a dozen feet into the living room, over the oak
table and its collection of "Give this to _____"; "Take this
when you go to _____." ... The sky is a deep blue after
morning fog, happy with itself for being so bright. I am hungry for
sun; I sit in the middle of a pale yellow rag rug on the living room
floor with Jasmine Pearl tea in a blue Fiestaware cup. I am catching
up, after two winters' darkness and snow. I am tired, but would
rather stay in the sun than lie down, even though the lying down
would be with cats.

December

My head marks me as someone who needs to be here—
sparse and absent hair; a suture line down the middle
of my skull:
I am among the sick for whom we will pray.
I settle into my pew, try not to weep too obviously.
I cannot speak the prayers without choking on tears:
I belong.

December 6

Parking Before CT Scan

The scan itself is a big nothing—
lots of lights in a circle around my head
but no noise,
no elaborate moving of the long table.
Just a lying still with lights.
It is over quickly.

But the parking beforehand is both nuts and sublime.
The signage is vague: Visitor Lot.
Well, I'm not a visitor. I'm someone
who is at the hospital for a test.
I back carefully out of the visitor lot and continue the circle
in front of the hospital and back to the visitor lot again,
scanning for somewhere legal to park.
Back at the visitor lot again I decide—in the absence of other
    options—
maybe I am sort of a visitor. I see nothing else
and I don't want to be late for what my doctor has called
an emergency CT Scan. I pull in.
I can see it's going to be complicated.
Scattered about are large meters.

I park at the back right, looking for whatever meter
goes with my space.

Behind me I see something tall and metal.
I get out of my car and go to it.
A tall man is trying to figure out
what to do with the meter, talking himself
through the directions, which—
because of the angle of the sun and the color of the reading
    screen—
are nearly invisible.
We shade our eyes, reposition ourselves against the light.
The cost is $1 for each thirty minutes.

The man pulls out a credit card.
I begin to fret about time: How long will this take?

Then: *Five dollars* he says. *I'll put in five dollars.*
He has decided on a bill rather than his credit card.

Touch any key for a receipt he reads aloud for us.
He touches a key, then reaches down for the receipt—
which he must then put inside his vehicle on the dashboard
or risk a ticket.
But he doesn't leave.

How am I supposed to know how long I'll be gone? I wonder.
It depends on the line in front of me
and how can I know that, standing here in the parking lot?

I am annoyed with the stupidity of this parking procedure.
There are little buildings where attendants once sat;
no one, now. *What price saving a buck?* I think.

I pull out four one-dollar bills, smooth their edges,
feed them in. The man waits, talking me through: straight edges:
Perfect!

The receipt comes out way below he reminds me.
You won't see it. You have to reach down and feel it.
It'll curl over.

He waits until I've got a receipt for my dashboard.
Flashes a wide smile.

We go to our cars, place our receipts, and then
begin the hike to the hospital's main entrance.

Not Ready for CT Scan

Yesterday when I heard about the CT Scan I thought
I'm not ready! (if I am entering an endgame)
but I also know I'll never be ready.

I will write
and go to church and plant in the yard
and do laundry and visit with people
until the very end. I'll never
be ready to leave this life—
except I will be, of course;
but in terms of still having projects
I want to do and experiences
I want to have, I will not ever
be ready.

Perhaps being forced to cut to the chase
reminds me to let go of everything that isn't
most important.
Again, I could really use someone to step in
and help me with what *is* most important—and also
with what is middling.
Hope has thoroughly cleaned herself
and settled on my ankles.
Eliza has joined us, as well.

December 7

Time Zone Difference

I still sometimes live between:
East Coast time, West Coast time.
That three-hour difference still arises—
but thank God I am here
and not three time-zones distant
across that expanse of plain and
desert and high mountain.
I saw it all
and it was beautiful
and thank God I am here
instead.

To Whom to Give Stoles

Waking slowly this morning,
a light on in the study,
the cats still drowsing,
I plan to whom to give my stoles.
There are three I love most:
the bright red Christmas one
I sewed from Guatemalan table runners—
Mary can match its joy;
the earth-celebration one in greens and yellows and blues—
my "main" stole: It fits with David's solidness;
the woven rainbow of bright colors—
Cathy's height can carry its length and her exuberance
its exuberance.

My clothing—fitting me—is likely too small
to go to friends and colleagues;
and much of my furniture too large
for others to take; and books are impersonal;
but my jewelry and artwork and smaller possessions
I want to have loved, close homes
with people I have loved.

December 8

Sense of Loss

Getting out the hammer to hang the framed painting of a cat
sitting on a chair, turning on the hot water faucet to rinse a plate,
sweeping the side porch,
I sense I have misplaced or lost something precious and not to be
    replaced—
lots of money,
one-half of the pair of my favorite turquoise earrings,
the blue and brown Tree of Life weaving found more than twenty
    years ago in Evanston,
the hand-painted Guatemalan E and K alphabet letters,
the rose clock,
the girl at the top of the tree waving her hands to a rooster.

I unpack more boxes and find these; or—in the case of the earring—
just before I vacuum, luckily I spy it
lying upside down on the rug near the front door, its silver visible
but its turquoise concealed in tufts of brown rug.
I had spent the morning on which I lost it calling every place I had
    been
and then driving there to physically look for it.
Thank goodness it fell from my ear to softness
rather than seconds later on leaves and concrete outside.

In all I unpack, miraculously only one thing is irreparably broken:
a brown pottery jar given by Anne years ago for Christmas or a
    birthday.

Likely it was a private potter, not commercial,
not terribly strong material.
I had recently mended its top after accidently dropping it.

Finally I realize: Of course I keep feeling like
I've lost something major and not to be replaced.
I *have* lost much. Much will not be replaced. This is accurate;
my visual memory is so challenged that I *am*
constantly misplacing things, not seeing in my mind's eye
where I last used or left them.
I've lost: the extra rent extorted by Chad
right after I got out of the hospital;
the clothing that did not make it from
NICU to a regular hospital room. And:
my health and profession
and financial standing,
a very large number of people
and a program and an assistant I loved.
Plus very nice neighbors and a good area for walking.
The mistake is in *thinking* I have lost something
rather than remembering with certainty;
and in thinking the loss in objects
rather than my body, the ephemeral, the more-than-real.

Lesser of Two Evils Gratitude

I am subject to this lesser-of-two-evils
backing-into thanks—the gratitude of

at least difficulty with time isn't so bad as losing
language ability.

I do wonder, though:
Is it still really thanks,
or a whiny sort of *Well, if something* had *to happen . . .* "—

trying to be a good sport about what I would prefer
not happen at all.

Both are true: The thanks is genuine
and it's thanks-with-a-caveat

which perhaps is fine.

If I'm about practicing wholeness,
surely that includes saying
what I really wish.

More About Luck

Surely there is some elegant luck
at play in my having difficulty
with time sequence and numbers
but not language.

Poet that I am,
a deficit in language
would have been devastating
but
numbers—

when I never was avaricious
or plotted a career
by what I could earn
though perhaps I should have—
numbers are troublesome
but not essential.

Perhaps some vast intelligence
took this into consideration,
even though I declare the tumor
not an act of God except in the most tidal wave,
tsunami, earthquake-like manner.

And so my prayer of gratitude:
I give thanks that if something
had to be troublesome now
it is not words, syntax,
meaning,
but the adding and subtracting of *amounts*—
conveyed by symbol and sequence rather than metaphor
or listening for what wants to be said.

December 15

After Visiting with a Colleague

After a time with my colleague and after we part,
I notice I do not feel bouncy and energetic.
I feel sad. I think this is not about my colleague

but my tumor and having left ministry:
My life is no longer like his life.
I am grieving loss.

Later, I am still sad:
Sadness has descended on me like night.
Everything feels too hard.
The procedure for changing the address on several magazines
is not apparent in the beginning pages of the magazines themselves
and when I finally find a website for one of the magazines,
      it wants to
charge me nearly $10 to make the change. The hotel that out
      of the blue
charged my debit card last week must be contacted directly; my
      credit union cannot refuse
a charge from it. I must go back online and track down
a number for the hotel—something I tried to do,
without success, earlier today.

December 19

First Visit to Saint Martin's

My head marks me as someone who needs to be here—
sparse and absent hair; a suture line down the middle of my skull:
I am among the sick for whom we will pray.

I settle into my pew, try not to weep too obviously.
I cannot speak the prayers without choking on tears:

I belong.

I am in the right place—which I knew as soon as I walked in and
saw the heading on the bulletin:
*The Episcopal Church of Saint Martin: Where you can find God—
and God can find you.*

I like this, although until recently I would have taken exception to
        finding God
specifically in a church rather than Everywhere.
I like God finding me. I need that.

I am sitting on the right side, two-thirds of the way back—
rather hidden, not conspicuous: cover for my head—
therefore for *me*.
I am sneezing—as unobtrusively as possible—
from an allergic reaction to I know not what.
I have been sneezing since I got to Davis six weeks ago.

The rector is on his game:
During the passing of the peace, he smiles at me
and then comes directly to me: a new face.
He holds out his hand.
I like him already.
He asks if this is my first time visiting.

I shake my head no.

I visited about eight years ago

I tell him, remembering that summer before seminary.
Really, it is more—more than eleven years.

Later, walking in dusk in the greenbelt,
remembering the morning,
I compute the years.

After the passing of the peace, the woman sitting two yards
down from me overexudes about the beauty of
my periwinkle-colored coat. I realize she needs something to say
rather than comment on my hair, my head.
So do I.
I nod and smile, wanting to be friendly in return.

Later I email to Mary and David that I have found a heart-fit here.
Unitarian Universalism is an intellectual fit—which is big,
but not big enough.
I think the question is how to make Episcopalianism
intellectually a fit.

The day after Christmas I email the rector, later thinking
Sheesh! He's busy enough. I should have just called the office.

    Is there a membership class or path toward membership?

He writes back that same day.
Not until spring. But do call me if you would like to talk.
We welcome all who are seeking to know the Divine.

He already knows that I am an ordained UU minister
and have cancer.
And he is not afraid.

December 26

Christmas Eve, Part One

I didn't recognize you! she says
when I give my name and hold out my hand.

It is night, but that isn't the reason.
We are near the church entrance.
She is greeting.

She is not embarrassed by her rudeness—
may think she is simply being honest:
I have fooled her.

My face is rounder; my hair is quite a bit shorter

I say, helping her out
so that the dark around us is filled with more than a knifing.
Later I think I should stop doing this.

She follows up rudeness with invasiveness.

Are you on Prednisone?—asking what drug I am taking
as though ice cream flavor preference.

No

I say, and say the name of the steroid I *am* taking.
I have not started to tackle this form of rudeness yet—
still new and breathtakingly surprising to me.
We have not said to each other

Let's talk about what drugs we are taking.

I've not asked her if she is taking something
to help her through menopause or with high blood pressure.

I realize she is looking for something known
to which to attribute my change in features.
Someone else she knew took Prednisone and got a fat face.
I chuckle, which loosens up some of her intensity.

I do not volunteer that on the top and on the right side of my head
I have almost no hair at all
or that I have a thin scar down the center of my head
and my head is bumpy (would she like to feel it?) from how my
    skull has
settled after removal of a large tumor
and black stitches are still visible at the crown,
five and a half months after surgery.

I am reminded of the woman's first name.
I knew her a dozen years ago.

Hello, _____! I say again. Given her first name
(the other woman near us says it),
I retrieve from memory her last name,
which I offer. She nods. I am correct.

If I had been burned on my face or lost an arm or leg
would she say

I didn't recognize you!

Likely no. She would find a way to cover.

Here's the cover:
Just say hello—as in

Hello! Nice to see you (tonight/this morning, _____).

True, I look different with a fatter face and little hair,
 but—help me out here—is it kind to draw attention to this
as though I am now an unknown?

No.

Listen up.

Here's what you need to do:

Keep your surprise to yourself.
Swallow it. Aloud say something else.

Graciousness is never out of place.

December 28

Christmas Eve, Part Two

The Presbyterians relate a coherent, linked story:
God sends an angel to tell a young girl she will conceive
and bear God's child—a son.
The girl says *Who? Me?*
Okay—with Your help.

The girl and her husband-to-be travel a great distance
in order to be counted for the ruler's tax.
When they get to the man's home town, Bethlehem,
the baby is born—which causes great joy in heaven.
Angels sing to shepherds who are in the fields with their sheep.
The shepherds go to the town to see the newborn child,
who—they've been told—
has been born a king.

Words to the songs are shown on a large screen set up
on the chancel. We stand for singing some hymns;
sit for others. Children are invited to bring up to the altar
representations of things we are singing about: angels,
Mary and Joseph, the baby, manger animals, shepherds.
They'd been allowed to choose among these as we entered.
The screen shows the story: the angel announcing the birth,
the young girl, the week's journey to Bethlehem,
the closed door of the inn, the stable and manger,
the newborn baby, the angels,
the shepherds with their sheep.
All is a whole: a story with a beginning,
a middle, and an ending.

There are Christmas greens about
with tiny white lights. Also a Christmas tree,
lighted in white. But no attempt to tie in the greens
and tree and wreaths. The focus is just the story.
The service is lay-led, not a minister in sight.

The Unitarian Universalists are all over the map. Six or seven
    sections,
a minister in stole and academic colors,
some four hundred participants,
themes that start and stop,
the only consistency the lighting of small candles
(for darkness and mystery, justice and giving,
hope for all the world)
across the top of the pulpit.

One hapless college student,
finishing a personal reflection,
knowing he should light a candle and
not seeing quickly in his order of service the reason why
calls out—
And now we light a candle, for—for what?

    Someone calls back
    For Jesus!

Oh, yeah: for Jesus.

He lights the candle and sits down.

There is even a dance at the end.
Two little girls who have been wiggling
and whispering and hanging on and within
the bars near their seats near me
dance a tale of bringing an old woman
out of her separation from others
and the world. The girls are serious about

how they step down the ramp,
how they twirl and turn,
how they bend down to lift the woman's
brown veil and help her stand.

There is plenty of music: two college-age trumpeters,
singing of carols by the congregation,
singing by the choir in harmony, in unison,
in solos, the choir director serious in high black heels
and short black dress.
Plenty of words:
careful designation between secular and sacred,
a prayer, invitation to the offering. Some silence.
Something to appeal to every manner of learning—
auditory, kinesthetic—and every stance
about the meaning of Christmas.
And all of it is disconnected: There is no single,
heartfelt *story*. The circle is so wide
there is nothing in it; there is no one
who says of the event: I own this in its entirety.
I am exhausted: too many leaps and holdings;
too many exceptions.

Can't we for once just read the Bible as it is? I think.

I had thought to go home for a bit and then go to the
11:00 PM Episcopal service, but in the dark parking lot
the locks of my car misbehave in the cold, refusing
for a time to open. Luckily, someone near has a flashlight.
I cannot imagine being stuck outside my locked car

at midnight on Christmas Eve on an empty street
in front of the Episcopal church,
even if it is near Trader Joe's.
Regretfully, I drive home and stay home.
I think the Episcopalians would have told a coherent story
complete with choir and pipe organ.

December 30

Not a Massage Therapist

A woman whom my doctor has recommended
as a massage therapist tells me over the phone,
never having met me, a minute into the first conversation
we have ever had

You should have a mantra:
I am cancer-free and I deny having it.

This, based on the tumor having been removed—
which she asked (*Did they get it?*) and I told (*Yes*).
She has at last returned my call of several weeks ago.

What gives her the right to assess my state of cancer
or non-cancer;
and what right to proclaim for me
a focus for my living?

True, she may believe she gets only one
chance to save me and this is it, talking to me now—

but

how dare she not simply ask if there is an affirmation
that appeals to me?

When we believe in something, it manifests

she continues.

Great.

Meaning that years ago when
this cancer got its start
I *believed* I had cancer?

I'm not pushy

she says.

I'm just here to facilitate
something that works.
Pick a mantra, and before you get out of bed
in the morning, work on it.

I can treat you in support of your being cancer-free.

When there is opportunity for a gracious leave-taking,
I tell her good-bye.

January

When I am writing now
or working on parts of this book,
it's the purest happiness I've ever known.
It's like I go to play in some sweet realm where there is
only listening for one word and then another,
only listening for what is true and deep.

January 1

What's Your Prognosis? UCD Campus Version

What's your prognosis?

Finally the question comes respectfully,
carefully, even tenderly.

I am stepping onto a sidewalk from a street on campus.
_____ and I are walking toward a bench we see in the sun.

Lousy

I say—because this isn't a cancer one expects to beat.
One day, it will win out.

I follow this up with

My surgeon cried—

which is perhaps not 140-percent accurate
but close enough.

He *looked* like he was crying.
He looked like he wanted to roll into
a tiny ball and get lost in a corner of the room.
He could not hold my gaze.
Inside, he was sobbing.
Grade four, after all that brilliant work
and my being (in his words) "one of the nicest people."

I say a bit about what *lousy* means—
statistics were avoided and
I was encouraged to avoid them, myself—
and say also

I'm aiming for another twenty years.

We sit in the sun and eat.

I keep exclaiming

This is SO GOOD!—

Sauteed mushrooms and onions and tiny tomatoes.

Then carrots and broccoli with feta cheese and pepper flakes.

He eats salad with what looks like fifty kinds of vegetables.
I am touched that he brought real forks and napkins for us
to pair with our take-out.

We talk—parents, families, how close in months we are
to our siblings, the need for a separate self.

Finally I say

On a day-to-day basis, I'm having a great time—

meaning

I'm not in any pain,

I get to go for walks in the greenbelt,

I get to write,

I get to be with friends.

No one asked in just this kind way before.

He did say as we set our things on the bench

It's kind of hard to ask that—

I think meaning how personal a question it is.

January 2

Bookshelf Story

I am making space on my study bookshelf
for the binders that hold my book draft.
All of the binders are recycled.
I have labeled them carefully by month
in the clear, easy-to-read printing style
I learned from watching my mother print in
indelible black ink on cardstock
for the bulletin boards she made for her kindergarten,
first- and second-grade classes.
Earlier I had carried out to the kitchen
the paper and binder files that had been stored here,
got out the ladder, and lifted these older files to
the cupboards above the sink—a balancing act
for which I took off my shoes
and wore only Mary's purple and lime-green
spotted socks on my feet

and stepped carefully so as to miss
the pot-filled sink.

As I place the binders in their new bookshelf home
my eyes fall on these titles, all standing right near each other:
Your Perfect Right: A Guide to Assertive Living;
Practicing Right Relationship: Skills for Deepening Purpose, Finding
     Meaning, and Increasing Effectiveness in Your Congregation;
The Essential Enneagram: What's Your Path to Happiness? The
     Definitive Personality Test and Self-Discovery Guide;
Brain Rules: Twelve Principles for Surviving and Thriving at Work,
     Home, and School;
Pursuing Pastoral Excellence: Pathways to Fruitful Leadership;
Wanting Wholenesss, Being Broken: A Book of Sermons;
Transforming Words;
Finally Comes the Poet.

Perfect.

These are my story: quite remarkably arranged
without my doing:
I wanted to live, needed to live,
more assertively in relationships that give back
what I give (my perfect right is this);
now—unexpectedly and unasked—
I have entered new rules for my sweet brain,
new understanding of pastoral excellence,
new embrace of who I am.
Now I am visibly significantly broken.
I am also quite whole:

Finally the poet steps out
and cannot stop stepping.

January 3

List Before Rising

In the morning before I actually get out of bed
I think of a dozen things to do first:
clean the litter box, put clothing away into closets,
clear off the dining room table, make space on the floor
of the walk-in closet and move in boxes from my study,
sweep the porch and pick up feathers in the larger yard,
wash dishes, put unused framed pictures beneath my bed,
wash a load of colored clothing and linens.
I tire myself, just imagining.
The feng shui of my small house defeats me over and over.
Time to throw out or give away more,
to make open space.
Lisa will call in an hour.
In the evening or afternoon I have acupuncture again.
On a scale of 1 to 10, my nausea is now about 4,
after several days and nights of 9 ¾.
Just the memory of this makes it rise again.

January 8

Communion Wafer Times Two

Today I received the wafer—
"the body of Christ, the bread of heaven"—
twice. Not because I thought it out that way
but I was lost in thought and did not
draw my hands back to my body
after the first wafer.
Once I saw the second wafer coming—
this from an associate rector I like—
I decided to keep my hands out and accept it
rather than say I'd already received it.
He was in a rhythm.

Now I know what happens if one thinks too long
while kneeling, rather than rising and continuing to think.

Communion goes too quickly for me.
I'm not in the first set of people who get to kneel,
so I find a place from among those who have received
and gone back to their pew—which means not long to kneel
before someone comes with a wafer.
Perhaps what I need to do is not put my hands out
until I've settled my body and mind, so that
when they do go out, I am fully ready.
Of course, as an introverted Unitarian Universalist participating in
an Episcopalian rite, I've a lot of contemplating to do.

Fear Question

Gary and I are walking in Pittsfield Village.
He is on my right, intense—as usual.

Are you ever afraid?
he asks.

I consider. I think he means not just fear for my life
as from someone trying to assault me
but a general existential fear like a mist over everything
or one big something that comes in the night
and leaves me breathless.
Maybe something that men or parents feel more of—
like fear of not being able to provide for a family.

No, I'm not.

I have *been afraid in my life,*
but not now.

I turn to look at him. We keep walking.

And now—months later, having done the expensive and
life-necessary thing of moving to Davis I say

Well, yes.

But it isn't about the cancer
and what may happen to me as it progresses.
That I think I can handle.
I will be curious and I hope held in enough love that

I am equal to that. Plus I hope to wrest a good twenty years
before that.

I'm afraid about money
and having enough to see me through.

I saved diligently whenever I qualified via tax laws.
I can draw on those savings, but they will not last forever.
I have lived conservatively my entire life—
except starting this last spring
when I could no longer bear to stand and cook for myself
after forty years of steamed vegetables, brown rice, legumes,
nuts, a bit of dairy, and fruit.
I needed variety and someone else's efforts—
Chipotle, the Whole Foods salad bar.
Still need that.

In the absence of enough income to pay insurance premiums
($900 a month) and supposed incidentals—which are not
incidental but necessary to healing and thriving (acupuncture,
physical therapy, spiritual direction, psychotherapy,
whatever portions of intravenous and other treatments
my insurance does not cover)—

a welcoming waiting room is moot.

Fortunately I receive disability pay
and can receive it for up to five years
(statistically it's not expected I will live longer)
but the pay is 2/3 of my previous salary,
which was modest,
less than fair.

Treatment my doctor has ordered takes place each two weeks,
totals roughly $10,000 each time.
My insurance picks up most of this
but leaves out several hundred dollars.
Nearly half my income goes directly to medical care,
before
housing or food or transportation or the cats or charitable giving
      or fun.

Having cancer ought be enough of a life challenge.
I oughtn't face financial distress in addition.

Clergy Grief

As the clergy and service participants walk down the aisle
in the recessional, grief grips me.
I notice congregation members turning to face this group
as it passes—a gesture of respect.
I had been engaged in another kind of respect:
eyes on hymnal, fitting unfamiliar words to a
semifamiliar melody.
The thought of *never*—as in never again might I myself recess
after leading a service—fills my eyes with tears.
I blink furiously so that I don't actually cry.

I would like to sing forever—something
simple and easily known—so that I might sing myself into
I can do this.

The question is answered: It is not

only in the presence of colleagues of my tradition
that I experience grief,
but, apparently, in the presence of any colleagues
doing what I would love to do.
Fear about my financial situation takes a back seat to grief.

January 10

Justice

The top layer of her letter is all piety.
Underneath: sheer hardness of heart,
lack of heart, intent to demean and hurt.
I do not confuse the two.

I want to think that
living within her skin
is punishment enough:
No one can add to whatever hell
makes her cruel, sadistic, unkind.
And yet:
Justice would be so sweet.

Letting go of wanting justice
is not for the other,
who does not deserve more kindness,
but for me: that I be
as unencumbered as possible
by the snags and thorns of this world.

I owe her nothing;
gather all possible riches for myself.

Justice is complex:
not a matter of equity but patient waiting;
not the decision of evil ones but an outgrowth of trust
in personal integrity;
not ever one quick step but years of metaphor
lived consciously.

And there is lots of letting go.

January 12

Roses on Path

My walking features a rose.
Brisk pace, cool air, dogs
on leash and not
and a white rose on the far side
of this expanse of greenbelt.
Two petals tinged at their top with pale pink
but all else creamy white.
The rose comes after the path between houses to Quail,
after the avenue of trees,
after Impala,
after a stand of pines.

I always say hello.
Pause, bend, close my eyes,
bury my face,
inhale.
And a second time.
There are other roses further down—
pink, not so near the path.
I marvel: mid-January; blooming roses.

On another path home
between two driveways
stands a row of white roses
and one of yellow.
I stop to smell these, also,
usually two of each.
The single white rose has a stronger,
more rose-like scent
but the yellow and white will do
when this is my day's path.
I breathe deeply.

January 13

Writing Anger

I am in a time of writing
not eloquence or simple observation
but anger—which in theory
does not distress me

but I fear
it may distance others
who think it may fall on them
and they want to avoid it.

Not Everyone Doesn't Recognize Me

As I go into the credit union downtown
I see a window sign for a new independent bookstore:
Logos: *Used and Hard-to-Find Books.*

Darn! I think: *And Sweetbriar Books just went out of business,*
But it was over by the Co-op.
Too bad it didn't have this location.

I decide to explore the store after I make a return down the street.

    Nancy?

The woman I am approaching—who is seated
at a small table near the wall near the back of the bookstore—
speaks to me. I am wearing
my knee-length plum-colored winter coat and jeans,
but not my lime-green hat.

Surprised, I nod. Then my own question:

Chris?

She nods, still assessing: Is it really me?

We've not seen each other in perhaps fifteen years.
I step toward her, around the table, my arms wide.
She stands; we hug.
We had been close.
I notice that her hair is thin over her head.
I feel both surprised and disappointed—for her, for me:
It's so long after her own chemotherapy must have ended,
and still her hair hasn't grown back.
What does this bode for my own sparsely settled head?

> *Are you back?*

Yes. I came a couple months ago.

> *I didn't know. Are you in your old place?*

Yes.

I do not say why I returned; realize she may
deduce why.

I tell her what I am looking for—
Matthew Fox's *Original Blessing*.

> *This is my first five minutes* she says.
> *I'm afraid I don't know where to look.*

A woman who seems to be the owner steps in to assist.
I follow her to several shelf areas where the book might be found.
I imagine Chris is following me with her eyes, thinking.
I feel protective of my head and its story;
realize I do not just easily say

I have cancer, so I came back.
I transferred my treatment to the medical center.

For one thing, I do not know whether to say *had* or *have*.
Also, this is a public space
and my life is private.

Returning to Chris—which is what I want to do now, more than
  find the book, I say:

Do visit!

I write out for her how to contact me.
I have her old number and email address.

I hope she does call.

January 17

How improbable is that?

says Mary when I tell her I seem to be dating _____.

We are setting off for a walk in the greenbelt.
Mary has come to visit
within a visit to Oakland and San Francisco.
We last saw each other five months ago.

How improbable, indeed! And how utterly right
and wonderful.

I told Julie last summer I thought I would
emerge from cancer partnered.

She was surprised but I said *Look.*
There is a power in the cancer, a cleanness
that protects me.

The pretend and the young fall away.

Offer

In the evening, driving to my home and then parking
after the concert, you say

Please ask me if there is anything you need done—
like cleaning the gutters or moving the armoire.

Just this afternoon, you had surprised me with the gift
of cleaning the gutters.

Okay

I say, though I am tempted to try to clean the gutters—
good, satisfying outdoor work
that has an immediately visible and household-friendly result
and is done from a ladder at enough height
to invite a little wooziness.
I am not so ambitious as to try to move the armoire—
though I did speak of moving it (never meaning I would try it
    alone)

before I got the couch and evened out
the bulk of big things in the living room.

These are the things I've come up with so far
with which I could use your help:
the boards that once were shelves along the study wall
wrangled into lying down in the attic;
the potted lemon tree tilted onto the wheeled plant caddy
so that I can move it out from under the porch overhang for
    sunlight and rain
and move it back again for protection from frost;
the lid of the pickle jar unscrewed so that I can add dill pickle to
    tuna.

And (these are more mind than muscle):
Please: Teach me everything you know about the iPhone;
please teach me everything you know about editing a document on
    the computer;
help me find the poem file *Fear Question;*
go with me, as you offered, to visit my parents.

I have creatively enticed bags of potting soil, bags of compost,
    garden bark, litter,
and cat food from the car and into the yard and house
and have finagled almond butter and vegetarian mayonnaise jars
    open
without straining my chest ligaments, somehow using just my
    arms.
I will continue to do what I safely can of such endeavors; but large

and unwieldy objects—the armoire (which is more than a foot and
    a half
taller than I and a half-foot wider and is *not* moving),
boards, lemon tree, too-tightly held jar lids—
I promise I will not attempt.

Thank you for such a thoughtful, body-friendly offer.

January 18

First Appointment, Spiritual Direction

I write well

I say by way of explanation. Then stop, embarrassed:
I must sound as though I am conceited.

I am seeking to explain why a publisher would
want to publish a book about my living through—
living with—this cancer.

I am speaking with my potential spiritual director.
I think she looks a little shocked.
I am glad her name is Nancy—not because it is my name
but because when she opens the door I think:
I could use another Nancy in my life.

I lost one recently.

What do you write about?

she asks.

Everything that happens.
There's so much that we don't commonly know about
long-term illness.
I can tell the day-to-day.
It will be for other clergy, for anyone who has cancer,
families, pastoral care groups,
anyone who loves someone who is ill.

Nancy recovers.

You have a gift

she offers.

I look directly at her. Agree:

Yes. I have a gift.

I don't say I know this
is what I was set on this earth to do—write—
but it's so. It's all part of
living what I know is holy,
which is what I most want.

I realize I'm not saying how
my writing connects me to God
but it's so important I can't do that
without bursting into tears,
and I've just met her.
Too soon to be all-out crying.

So I think.

You're really good at being silent
I say at one point.
I am luxuriating in roaming wherever I desire
in the silence in this room.
I glance at Nancy. She nods.
Yes, she is good at being silent.

My eyes are filled with the pines that fill the window.

I like the room a lot:
Maybe eight feet by eight feet.
A small heater to my right.
A length of fabric that looks like Marimekko
but Nancy tells me she got it at Ikea. This hangs
from ceiling to floor behind her rocker: green lines that
start and stop like labyrinth lines; three very large, bright red-orange
flowers with black centers.
They look like Georgia O'Keefe compositions
shouting: Look at me! Only me!

A stone-like black and gray placard that informs

Be Still
and
know
that
I AM

is placed exactly where I might have placed it
in a small space between the lower right edge of
a square window and the wall corner,

so that the corner and the window edge are part of the design.
There is a bookshelf with a pillow covered in what also looks like
    Marimekko fabric
and a companion pillow behind me in my own chair.

I'm fully Finnish
Nancy says after I exclaim

Oh, you've got Marimekko!—
which was the fabric of my eighteenth year
when I lived first in Ilomantsi, Finland, in the Karelia bulge
near the Russian border and then outside Tampere at the edge of a
    lake
on which one could ski to town.

Nancy tells me when her father's family and her mother's family
came to the United States. Tells me

Finnish was the language spoken in both of my grandparents' homes.

I like the fat plant growing in a pot on the floor.

The room has what it needs—
including a pale blue rug patterned in softly colored bouquets
that connects the space between my chair and Nancy's rocker—
and not more.
It is a space of useful things
kept and reused.
Not ostentatious, not
things purchased
for one endeavor only.

I take in the small finger labyrinth
and the plate of objects one might
put in the small sand tray.
Also the two dark-green, tiny flower-blossom-like succulents
in identical white square pots; and
a lighted glass waterfall fountain.
Three places where there is light—
perhaps like the trinity, it occurs to me now.

Once I begin, I talk
nearly nonstop.

Yes!

I say at the end when Nancy asks
If I would like to work with her.
We agree: three to four months,
once a month.
We set a February appointment.

I go to Trader Joe's to buy bananas and brightly colored
bell peppers.

January 21

Lunch Is Broccoli

Lunch is broccoli, red bell pepper, mushrooms, and tofu cubes
cooked with sesame seeds and pepper flakes in vegetable broth;
jack cheese sprinkled over the whole.

Lunch is also telling important things: his siblings' names and birth order; where they live now. His children's names and ages; where they live.

Lunch is a few chores: turning over the glass table top, lifting the potted lemon tree onto the plant caddy, assessing whether I have a viable phone line (maybe not), unscrewing a jar lid, trying to ascertain why my space pen does not work.

Lunch is my eyes filled with his hand
wanting my own skin bare from elbow to finger tips, also
and lying by his.

Lunch is a hug good-bye
wishing it were not yet good-bye but accepting.
Delight in his saying he had a good time.
I did, too.

He goes to take up laundry again.
I go to walk in the greenbelt.

January 26

Love as the Sum

This is what I think about
the sum of the world being love:
It isn't,
in any usual daily experience
for most people;

but it *is* the way through, the way out,
when mayhem and hard things happen.
Love isn't usually *method*, but it *is* often conscious
process after unconscious or
could-have-been-avoided
hurting.

January 31

I was getting psyched up to take Temodar tonight, but it hasn't
arrived. Spent forty-five minutes trying to determine what
happened. Looks like there has to be a double okay each time—
from my physician's office, from me. The pharmacy doesn't appear
to be set up to work well with a schedule that is periodic rather
than continuous. I scheduled an extra acupuncture appointment
to help me through the Temodar. I'll keep it, even if I can't start
tonight, as possibly it is helping me perk up after having been
pretty sick with nausea and whole-body, flu-like achiness Saturday-
Sunday-Monday. Yesterday I just plain lay in bed from ten o'clock
on, watching children's programming until I went to acupuncture.
Possibly, if not tonight, I can begin the Temodar on Wednesday.

The young man I spoke to at the pharmacy was sweet. *I
understand! I'd be calling every day if I didn't have my medication.*

I'd asked *Do I have to call each time, in addition to my doctor's office
calling? Seems like duplicate work.*

I didn't receive a clear answer.

Happy

Mary and I are going to lunch.
She is visiting for the day from an event in San Francisco.
I am driving us in Davis.
I say something I don't quite mean to say:

I've never been happier—
in spite of the cancer and what it's meant.

I hadn't in good introvert form thought out this revelation
before I said it,
but once it's out
I don't take it back,
partly because Mary seems to like it a lot
and also because it's, well . . .
true.

In the weeks since, I've recalled this,
holding it up to the light from a number of angles.

The truth is: When I am writing now
or working on parts of this book,
it's the purest happiness I've ever known.
It's like I go to play in some sweet realm where there is
only listening for one word and then another,
only listening for what is true and deep.
That rests me. That heals me.

The truth is also that when I am walking in the greenbelt,
I am only walking in the greenbelt, even if I am walking briskly

and thinking to be home in forty minutes. It is pure joy to walk
    fast
and feel my lungs and feet and legs and arms
all enjoying this ensemble work we do.

In the weeks since my blurted joy to Mary,
I have remembered that careful, tentative, scared,
less-humid-than-usual June-July-August-September in Ann Arbor
    after surgery.
My body figured out then how to string together a number of
    blocks at a time, walking.
It was arduous work, beautiful though the trees were, soft as the air
    was.

I remember that hard summer with tenderness—for my tiny,
    lavender-painted
bedroom and the cards it held,
the lushly-planted neighborhood,
the kindness of my neighbors,
my daily flower gathering in the garden,
the way the cats and I curled in sleep,
the kindness of the congregation, excellent medical care,
the constant effort my body made to return to wholeness,
Bach that invited sleep, and letting go into unexpected, enormous
    change.

I am becoming rested now in a way I haven't been perhaps since
I went to Finland after high school and then returned home to
junior college and then transferred to Davis and the quick run of
my life since, which most recently included nine moves in eleven

years, three of them from one coast to the other in whiplash fashion.

So yes, I've never been happier:
in a fight for my life, and happy.

February

It isn't love that makes the world go round
but compassion—starting over in gentleness
when love hasn't been enough or other factors have failed:
a gentle refusal to blame oneself or others
and just begin again.

February 2

Imagining a Display of the Turtle and Horse Cards

Another layer of imagery:
turtle (with an ace bandage and two affixing clamps)
horse (the woman was not planning to ride, but will).

Something slow and within water;
something swift over ground and through air.

Something that meets little resistance;
something that constantly hits limits of rock, lungs, sinew.

Animal;
human.

All one wild, beautiful mix with a light-green background:
inherent, ongoing life.

February 4

Late January Temodar

Taking Temodar
(chemotherapy done at home)
can be a bit complicated.

I realized during the early morning hours
that I erred last night,
taking only one pill rather than three

when I got up at 7:20 PM to take the Temodar
(already sleeping after a rigorous week
and both physical therapy and acupuncture that day)
after having previously gotten up to take the preparatory
antinausea pill.
Given the level of distress I experienced last round,
I can be forgiven that forgetting.
I decided, still sleeping, there is nothing to do
but continue the next four nights
and add a sixth at the end when I take the remaining two pills.
The pills are huge—three-quarters of an inch long and a quarter-
    inch wide—
innocently colored pink and white
like a young girl's room.
But how treacherous!
They make my poor gut fold over itself in distress.
No wonder I slept without nausea last night:
only one-third the usual stew.
Seems simple enough,
but not even the pharmacy got it right this time,
saying on the label instructions to take the pills before breakfast.

No—it's two hours after dinner I take them
I had said over the phone when a young man called to verify the
    order (it's mail order for cost savings).

   Then I can't send it out.

Look it up
I ask.

It's always been two hours after dinner. Then it's two hours more
    before I can eat again. Not before breakfast.

He can't find previous information.
Refuses to proceed with the order unless my physician's office
    verifies my version.
Another day passes. No prescription arrives.
My doctor's office calls: *Sorry about the prescription snafu.*
The pharmacy made an error and will be calling me.

The pharmacy calls only to say in an automated voice
the prescription is on its way,
meaning I can start this round three days later than I might have.

I am surprised that when the prescription arrives it still carries
    incorrect orders.
So far this round it's taken me an hour and a half of telephone calls
to get the prescription sent.
I decided not to mess with getting the instructions corrected:
I know what they are.
Not worth another three-quarters of an hour to get them printed
    correctly.

More About Love

It isn't love that makes the world go round
but compassion—starting over in gentleness
when love hasn't been enough or other factors have failed:

a gentle refusal to blame oneself or others
and just begin again.

February 11

My Thoughts Escape

My thoughts escape over and over again
to the relationship that has failed.
I have said no to it in any form—
unhealthy for me to have any part of it—
but total *no* is so hard!
I want to argue that perhaps he will suddenly change:
only one woman at a time.
Then, maybe?
But how likely is that,
and how would I know?
He suddenly comes calling, once he is free?
I see some remaining issues, even were this one solved.
They are minor, in comparison.
At the moment, I can't begin to open the door,
let alone speak, after.

February 12

November

I have lost November.

Spring, June, July, August,
September, October, December,
January, February, and Empty
stand side by side on the bookshelf.
Inside the shelf cupboard doors
are empty binders; manila and colored files,
pocketed and plain;
tablets waiting to be written upon;
my first laptop and its case;
used and unused large manila mailing envelopes.
But no November. I check September,
October, and December carefully. No
intermixing, right? Right.
I check the cupboards above the kitchen sink.
No confounding of current writing with that of
ten and twenty and fifteen years ago, right?
Right. I check the desk and table tops.
No black or periwinkle binder hidden under papers, right?
Right.

November is nowhere.
I have no memory of having removed her contents,
no memory of a latch opening and everything simply spilling out,
no memory of taking her anywhere, loaning her, abandoning her.

If I must, I can simply print out
everything with a November date—
or collate all the other poems and see what's left out.
These, by elimination, will be November.
So she isn't entirely lost, except for any updating not yet entered.
Just badly lost for the moment,
lost to my touch and sight,
lost from her sister months,
lost from easy context.

Perhaps one more example of my not seeing
exactly what is in front of me.

February 15

Hair, Yet Again

My hair is beginning to grow back in—wispily, softly curling.
There's a grey-brown three-quarter-inch fringe across my
forehead—something like a friar's fringe. The back of my head
looks mostly filled in and so does the right side, where the temple
piece of my glasses had scraped away substantial hair. Even the
hair on top of my head over a main suture area is wispy and curly.
After I shower, my head looks a little like a wet duck head: unruly
feathers. The left side and top of my head are still mostly very
lightly settled, and the suture lines itch, itch, itch. I scratch ever
so gently—not back and forth but in tiny little straight lines after
which I pick my fingers up and then make more straight lines with
my fingernails again. Some of my hair is grey or white and straight

but mostly it's rich brown with some variety of curliness. I love how soft and baby-like it is. Mostly I go about without my hat now, except if I'm walking or to protect against cold.

February 28

Car

Roger* and I are walking north on S Street, downtown Sacramento,
looking for my car.
Numbered streets go from north to south;
lettered ones, east to west, following the early grid near the river.
I know my car is on the west side of the street,
but I don't remember which block or how far down the block.
After each block we pass
all I can say is

Well, not this one.

We are walking on the side opposite from where my car will be.
We look across the street for it.

Once, a week before I left Ann Arbor,
I parked somewhere between
the old heart of town and the hospital
without noting where or even in which direction the car faced
or which side of the street as I scurried to pick up a homeopathic
    remedy

*a colleague of Nancy's in California

and finally had my fill of one-way streets and took the first open
space I saw.

Then I spent an anxious near-hour searching for my car, trying to
walk with an even gait even though I was past tired, trying to be
compassionate with my inattentiveness. At home, I was packing to
move across country. I generally didn't walk for almost an hour;
particularly without a choice to stop and without my bed close by
for falling into whenever I wanted.

Today, I know in general where my car is: somewhere between
wherever I left it on S Street and Temple Coffee and Tea at the
corner of S and 29th, where Roger and I have just drunk very good
green jasmine tea poured from identical little white pots into
identical wide white cups. It is good to be with him.

The sunshine is full, the day filled with blossoms and spring
warmth. I had walked only a few blocks to the tea shop; parking
before the shop because I saw open curb space.

Finally I recognize three brightly-painted flats: the first one gold,
the middle one olive, the last one red-orange.

I drove by those!

I say happily.

But my car is not across from them, quietly waiting for me.

As we approach 18th Street, Roger asks

Did you go over the railroad tracks?

I study them, imagining: Did I? I'm not remembering their
   unevenness in my body.

No. I don't know if I went over them.
Oh! My sweet, sieve-like brain.

We wait while six light-rail cars pass; then turn back toward
Temple Coffee and Tea.

From the back, walking near it on the same side of the street,
finally I saw my car just after 26th Street. It was wedged in from
behind in a way it wasn't when I left it.

Roger and I had planned that if we didn't see my car by the time
we got to the cross street he was parked near, we'd go to his car and
continue the search with him driving. No need!

Later, driving home, I think

*Next time I'll search from the side of the street on which I parked.
And I'll leave extra room at the front for maneuvering out in case
someone parks too close behind.*

I come up with good ideas like this regularly now, as I try to
salvage something good from whatever has just gone awry.

I knew it wasn't very lost.
I was glad not to be walking alone.

February 29

Arguing Theology

Yesterday—the first Sunday in Lent—
for the first time I argued theology.
Didn't just let words pass over me and
enter the larger meaning, but argued

No, not mine

during the Great Litany
as choir members and clergy and other service participants
walked in procession down the center aisle to the chancel
and then down the right side and across the entryway
and up the left aisle
and back down the center aisle again.
Father Art sang the celebrant's words; the congregation
responded, all our words a chant.
What struck me: our asking—begging—for mercy from God, not
for a specific terrible offense, but more, it seemed, simply for the
fallenness or dirtiness of being at all. Then there *was* detail about
what we had done or what might befall us and that we sought
deliverance from.

I realized while I was arguing that I might have been particularly
sensitive to wording/theology that day because of having said yes
in the last several days to joining the congregation, so now what
I'm saying is not so much theory but claimed assent. I'd also spent
four hours the day before in a membership exploration session

with some attention to thoughtful naming of possibilities for the nature of God, all of which rational ones made good sense to me.

I had visions of my more knee-jerk anti-Christian UU friends voicing dismay at rather than acceptance of Episcopal theology.

I also felt judged by Father Ernie and his wife (projection?) when I announced after church at a gathering for potential members that I am a UU minister. *So why are you here?* is what I imagined I saw in their eyes.

I did not feel any desire to go into detail: *I've got cancer. I need to forgive a number of people for some things that seem egregious to me. Here, I am reminded that forgiving does not belong to me alone.*

By the end of the potential-member/potential-confirmand meeting I felt pretty separated from others. I'll continue with the process and try to be articulate the next two weeks at follow-up meetings.

March

I am more nearly
in the world without separation,
without cautious thinking.

March 2

Temodar

I am several days off schedule, due to the coordinating needed between the mail-order company and my doctor's office and the placement of the weekend in this. Were everything in place, I might have started this round on Monday.

The prescription arrived yesterday (Thursday) late afternoon. Even so, I'm considering not beginning it until Tuesday next week, so that I cannot, without additional nausea, work over the weekend on income tax, go to a choral concert with Libby on Sunday evening, and keep my appointment with Rev. L on Monday late morning.

It took such an effort of will to begin income tax that I am loathe to break the momentum. It's a completely different planet from working on the book, which work I think lights up the pleasure/ addiction centers of my brain.

Ideally, I wouldn't wait: simply begin the Temodar tomorrow if I've integrated Thursday's physical therapy well enough—but maybe the relief of finishing my part on income tax will compensate for any loss of chemotherapy "good standing" due to delaying a bit when I start on this round. I'm seeking to balance good effects.

March 7

Temodar Again

In the very early morning I wake enough to assess I've not taken the Temodar—which I deduce because my mouth is dry and I don't need to use the bathroom: I've not in the last few hours drunk three eight-ounce glasses of water, one for each large pill. I am disappointed, but not so much that I scramble out of bed and go take the damn pink and white things.

I wrestled mightily from 7 PM to 9:30 PM last night, to get up to take the pills, but drowsiness kept closing my eyes after a long day with two trips away from home. I was loathe to sit up into the wild dizziness I've had the last eight days, plus my legs would be cold until I got sweatpants or a bathrobe on. I cooled my head with a large ice pack under it and a smaller cervical one laid over it; and following that cooling, did lymph drainage work on my chest; I stretched my right shoulder girdle with the positioning Lisa had suggested in the morning, followed by heating my shoulder for 15 minutes that stretched to 25 because I was aching and the heat felt so good; I'd had in mind to do several other physical therapy exercises and even work for a couple hours on poems, but I couldn't wake up enough to get out of bed and go to the kitchen or my study.

I have to take the Temodar before I lie down in the evening
I said to myself. *Once I lie down, it's too hard to get up to take it.*

Good planning for the following days.
Didn't help me get up last night.

It was one o'clock the next morning—*this* morning—before
I realized I'd not gotten up. It still took a half hour to push
myself up (the dizziness was large but not wild, not huge, not
accompanied by vertigo) and go get a drink of water. I decided
before I got up not to take the Temodar during the daytime, as that
would likely blot out the entire day. Tonight I'll have to be planful
and alert, and take the Temodar at 7 PM without lying down before
that.

Last night, I bargained fiercely with myself, wanting to start this
round of chemo, not wanting to get up to do this. The comfort of
my bed won out.

I need to get started on this round of chemo.
It's cold and I'm tired.
I'm already a week late starting this round.
These blankets and pillows and quilts are soooo nice!

I should just get up and take the pills, cold legs or not. I can bring a
*   bowl and towels back to bed with me and throw up, if I need to.*
Maybe it won't matter if I'm a week late, or even if I don't take this
*   round at all.*
If I don't get started on this round, I could mess up my good record of
*   the tumor not progressing.*

Surely there's leeway in how precisely this chemotherapy is done
I said to myself.

Just get the first three pills over with.
I am so tired!

I knew if I were a child or teenager I'd be crying in protest:

*No! No! I don't want those awful pills. I don't want that terrible
     medicine!*

It's too early to get into such refusal. I've got at least ten nights to
go, and I'm afraid of wrecking the protocol if I don't immediately
get this round of five nights started and done. I walk this balance:
following the protocol set before me; huge aversion to how it
makes me feel. Deciding not to begin the Temodar so long as I was
coping with dizziness allowed me the leisure of a week apart from
increased nausea, a luxury for which I pay, now. I almost need
someone to come be with me while I take the damn things. That
person could then go home and let the cats take over.

March 10

Holy Man Dream

A holy man who is sitting with his hands clasped in front of him
says to the woman with whom he is sitting

You're fat!

He is serious, as though reporting
something obviously and completely true.

The woman is not fat. She is some twelve pounds heavier in the
     last nine months
but she is not fat.

She began this gain when she was just over a hundred pounds,
    none of this poundage
clumped in one spot.
She is, some friends say, looking better than before she needed
    extra calories to soften the harshness of chemotherapy.

Friends say
Finally some meat on her bones to anchor her in a large wind and
soften the boniness of hugging her.

So the question is:

fat with what?

Surely there is at least one very large thing:
    grief

    also fear
    and
    dread

She has about two more months of chemotherapy,
and in the last few days has been heartsick that perhaps the tumor
    has
silently, suddenly grown. She had been for all of one afternoon
    badly lost in an inexplicable time warp, numbers and lettered
    street names and her watch face meaning nothing easily
    discernible.

Is this the way it plays out?

she wondered, waking early the morning after that terrible being
    lost.

I just gradually lose more and more
cognitive ability and arrive at the right place
at the wrong time or miss a turn and don't arrive at all
because I'm lost on lettered streets that I can't find my way out of
when I come across them in reverse order?

So some fatness with grief, yes.
Also some with the box she can't figure out about her family.

They want to visit, but she hasn't the energy it takes for defending
     herself against
the huge sucking out of air and life that happens to her in their
     presence.
They mean only to make clear to her that they love her,
and for that love they include demands to her they can't perceive.

Fat with the impossibility of being the daughter they want *and* also
protective of herself.
Fat with grief and stress about that:
no way out.

March 22

White Lab Coat Dream

I am wearing a white coat that has shrunk.
I try it on, looking at myself in a mirror,
trying to remember its lines:
How small is it compared to
what it was before it was washed?

I decide it is not terribly much smaller,
but then I look at it from my right side
in the mirror. It comes just to my waist,
and I remember it had been much longer—
at least to my hips.

I try to pull it down.
I can stretch it down a little,
but not nearly enough
to be what it was.

Waking, I forget the dream
until lunch, when suddenly
I see in my mind that looking
in the mirror at my right side.

I see the dream this way:
My lab coat has grown
much smaller. I am more nearly
in the world without separation,
without cautious thinking.

March 26

Poem Written in Spring

Remove me from God and I wither,
stop my writing and I grow toxic.
The poison I take in must go somewhere.
Paper will do.

April

Here is where the new begins.

In April, Nancy began to lose function on the left side of her body and was hospitalized a couple of times. The tumor had begun once more to make its presence felt. Additional surgery to remove it was discussed, and ultimately rejected. The poems she wrote in this month were laboriously typed out one-handed; it seemed miraculous that she was able to finish any, and that the ones she finished were nearly as precise as the rest of her writings. In April and until the very last of her days, she continued to treasure life—visiting with friends, noticing beauty, caring for her two beloved cats, loving food, appreciating kindness from her caregivers—and also letting them know when they fell short in caring for her the way she needed. Among the April writings are included some of her emails, sent at all hours of the day and night. I have included them without correction, both as visual markers of the progression of the disease and also to bring light to the truly extraordinary effort she was making in bearing witness to the end of her life. This was the last month Nancy was able to write. In May, she entered hospice care.—MMG

April

I call Mary to tell her my left arm is losing function.
Finally I got to the computer to enter a poem
and my arm won't respond.
I sit watching my own demise.

I am going to need to get a stenographer to enter what I say.
I still see ways of writing—I dictate, for example—
and another person types it in.

But more, I want someone to just sit
and write what I say so that I can see it
and correct as needed.

So weird!
Finally I had the first real poem of this last week's adventure
and no way to make it appear.
At least my right hand still can use a pen—the old way now so
    much quicker
and less frustrating.
Who can write this down for me? Who can receive it?
More to work on, which I cannot do alone.

Hope has settled on my legs on the Placerville quilt.
All is well.

Mary assures me that the book will get done
    and crying is always fine.
    I assure her back.
    I put the heating pad over my esophagus,
    which is reporting I ate too much sushi too quickly
    and it wants to flee.
    I go to put Mary's spotted socks on my feet.
    They are what I am wearing when the toilet overflows
    so I have to take them off before Sonie* and I leave for the
    hospital.

* *Nancy's cousin*

From: Nancy Shaffer
Sent: Saturday, April 7, 2012
To: Mary McKinnon Ganz and David Keyes

david and nary,

i'm home , thank god, with some diminished capacity in my
left arm —what's a computer? it ASKS?— but basically still me.
need a smart assistant while the light is still on. my task for
today.

loe to you. -n

Fsulous to be home. Fabulous to be puttering in my own kichen
for chick pea with spinach salad anf Vittle Vitttles organic
cornbread tOAST AND GREEN TEA. DOABLE BUT REALLY
SLOW. ELIZA SITS AND EYES ME AS THOUGH SHE IS MY
TRAPRReZE SPOTTER. I CAREFULLY LEAN TO PET HER. IT
IS JUST AFTER 3 AM BUT MIGHT AS weLL BE FULLY THE
NEXT DAY. I DO NEED SOMEONE TO BE THE ME I AM NOT:
FINDING sPOONS, SETTING THE DISHWASHER TO RUN,
untangling the cord to the heavy wooden blinds my neighbor
has tightly wound up so that the cats will not tangle in it and
die. all of this in a calm race against time:what is the tumor
doing, and how quickly? HOw MUCH CAN I POUR OUT WHILE
STILL THTERE IS TIME?

emails may become poems . . . .

From: Nancy Shaffer
Sent: Tuesday, April 10, 2012
To: Mary McKinnon Ganz

a hard day, but done and now have had good dinner and will lie down with cats. income tax info needed for extension is with accountant —huge relief. light rain. didd you see more of herring run? get someone large to move the couch?*

From: Nancy Shaffer
Sent: Thursday, April 12, 2012
To: Mary McKinnon Ganz

Time and Me Now

I wake into that vast inter-stellular exchange land
where new days are agreed upon and earth shifts
and we agree to start over again:
a shiny new black sheet of time spread out for all to use.
What shall we name it?
Thursday?
Friday?
Wednesday?

* Refers to a telephone conversation the day before, in which I told Nancy I was hoping to see the herring when they were running in a stream near my house in Massachusetts, and that we were rearranging furniture at my house but could not manage the couch by ourselves. With all that was going on in her personal world, with her body deteriorating, as she said, before her eyes, Nancy was still remembering details of a friend's life. —MMG

I feel the shift
but am no any longer
part of its choosing.
I just accommodate to it,
whatever the agreement is:
Okay, now it's Thursday.
It's all the same:
I'm still hungry, still cared for, rested, warm.
I snuggle down into down pillows, soft sheets, small quilts.
It's all the same:
A day, any day
is good and welcomed:
one more, whatever it brings.

Do I want breakfast at 6 AM?
It's so much more complicated than that
and my awareness of my desires
and this living are so much more complex than that.
I *feel* that we are all somewhere else now but I don't easily feel
     where in days that new somewhere else is.

From: Nancy Shaffer
Sent: Thursday, April 12, 2012
To: Mary McKinnon Ganz

wrestled to ground!

Cats at Midnight

Suddenly, unexpectedly,
when I am weary beyond weary,
the cats have a restless night.
Eliza cries over and over in small pieces of cat-anguish
outside the door to my room,
which has gotten closed.
Hope —
usually a silent, simple circle of soft fluff—

Dashes periodically up and down the hall,
turning at the last minute right toward the study or left into my
    room
and then leaping onto the bed.
Her long fur swishing against the antique butter mold that now
serves as a narrow stand-alone shelf near the corner wall.
I keep trying to sleep through this.

Finally I decide there is nothing to do but get up, go to the kitchen,
    eat:
The cats will see that I am fine and calm down.
M turns on her side on the couch,
the light-green blanket
drawn over her shoulder and bent legs.
I stand at the counter and devour roasted chicken, rice porridge M
cooked for me in the afternoon, now cold:
kale and golden beet salad with cottage cheese pieces,
sparkling water that calms my esophagus.
All is fine on my end.

I return to my bed;
Eliza does not.
Again I think I know what comes next: sleeping.
Again I think I know the sequence:
waking rested and hungry,
finding the good food others have prepared for me,
returning to bed for more rest and seeking of the Sacred,
asking what stretching toward it is needed right now.

But how utterly physical the Sacred is!—
not the clean quiet, private holiness of prayer
but physical *doing:*
the body rather than the mind.

Even as I finally sit hours later now to try to type this,
Eliza comes to meow at me:
I must first return to bed so she can guard again.
Reluctantly, I rise,
My left hand now so slow.
What may it have lost by the time I sit again?
More stretching toward the Sacred.

I keep seeing the golden floor boards of the tiny Ann Arbor living
    room—
that morning beauty.

I love working during the night,
But how disorienting for others!

6:00 AM:

An insight I wake with: Perhaps I become my own assistant;
no separate writing any further,
but writing directly to the computer as thoughts come; one
    process.

Hope has melted herself into one of the 90-degree ledges of my
    bent knees,
ears and tiny cat-face a fluffy pure-velvet circle 12 inches across the
    white Episcopalian Placerville prayer quilt.

Eliza lies curled into a bright 18-inch half-circle of black, striped
    orange, and brilliant white
near my feet.
Eliza eyes me:
okay for me to get up now.
I step over the red-bound King's Chapel prayer book
with which I finally propped open my bedroom door for Eliza last
    night.

Time for tea.

From: Nancy Shaffer
Sent: Friday, April 13, 2012
To: Mary McKinnon Ganz

an amazinglt hard day, but ending much better than started. no
apparet progression.n

got to get help with dictating.n

storm has finally broken here.
so it feels with at last a good helper, i think. really hard to put
into place,

and my sweetest med center roommate called and said got
dinner plans? so i do..... love, n

When does an artist eat?
Asked as part of questions for providing 24-hour care.

Before during, after, creation of the art.
Whenever the art has declared itself
enough of a being that
that it will still be present
if eyes and time are taken for refreshment.
The eating is part of the creating—
the *real* emerging from its first nest:
taking in sustenance in order to focus on image,

feeling, the coming forth.
All of this is food, connection to primal impulse:
the *real* emerging from its nest.

The artist eats continuously,
no schedule possible.

All creating is listening.

From: Nancy Shaffer
Sent: Sunday, April 15, 2012
To: Mary McKinnon Ganz

More About Time and Me, Now, Remembering the Night

I wake in the nest of creativity,
the dead of night
when there is no agreement
what to call this vast new thing—blackness, time and origin
beginning again.
How I love the dark!

My altered sense of time and wakefulness
is not annoyance
but welcome glee.
Here is where the new begins.

This is the last poem Nancy completed. After this there were only emails and fragments of poems, many concerned with food and with getting her caregivers to understand her needs for nutrition. Nancy had spent her entire adult lifetime avoiding refined sugar, but toward the end of this month, she discovered chocolate, and then, Ben and Jerry's vanilla ice cream. "I am aware it is as though I am resetting life itself: everything possible good at the last minute," Nancy wrote on April 18. "I love this physicality, this glorious tasting while there is still time!"

Nancy died at home in Davis, California, on June 5, 2012, one year to the day after she was admitted to the hospital in Ann Arbor. Her death was peaceful. She was attended by her father and her mother, Lee and Marjorie Brooks, and by her caregiver, Asenaca Hussein. Earlier that evening she was visited by her minister, Rev. Beth Banks of the Unitarian Universalist Church of Davis, who sat with her more than an hour, sang to her, and read her the 23rd Psalm.—MMG

Reprise: Calling, Part Two

I begin to understand calling more fully.
It has little to do with ministry itself;
everything to do with the Sacred.
It is not about serving a particular denomination
or even congregation
but being in the world who
I was created to be—
like standing on the stage of the universe
and saying Yes to God alone and not
a particular mountain range or river.

After that, what possibly can go wrong?

Acknowledgments

It is impossible to give large enough thanks, on Nancy's behalf or on my own. This is a partial list of colleagues:

For being a magnificent minister to Nancy and to me, the Rev. Elizabeth Banks of the Unitarian Universalist Church of Davis.

For supporting Nancy in countless ways, financially and emotionally, and for supporting me in helping to care for her, the Rev. Richard Nugent, who administers the Living Tradition Fund of the Unitarian Universalist Association.

For supporting Nancy in ways including driving her to the emergency room, helping her afford the costs of her move, visiting her in the hospital and at home, and in ways I cannot know, the Rev. Gail Geisenhainer, the Rev. Mark Evens, and Sandy Garges of the First Unitarian Universalist Congregation of Ann Arbor, and other colleagues in Michigan.

For driving Nancy and her beloved cats, Eliza and Hope, across country to their home in Davis, for listening well, for her good suggestions in this work and otherwise supporting me in this project, the Rev. JD Benson, my partner in life and ministry.

For colleagues who visited her and supported her in the Pacific Central District, including the Rev. Leslie Takahashi Morris and the Rev. Roger Jones, and for visiting her in Ann Arbor, the Rev. Erika Hewitt.

For her friend, mentor and supporter of many years, the Rev. David Keyes, who edited her meditation manual, *Instructions in Joy*, and who consulted generously in the editing of this volume.

And for stepping forward with an unqualified "yes!" to be power of attorney, enabling the life-saving surgery to go forward, Cathy Harrington.

For the doctors, nurses, and technicians at University of Michigan Hospital, many of whom will find themselves in these pages, deepest thanks. Thanks also to the corresponding staff who took over Nancy's care at University of California Medical Center in Davis and Sacramento.

For the congregation and staff members who cared for her from the UU churches in Ann Arbor and Davis, and from St. Martin's Episcopal Church, profound thanks. A couple of names will have to stand for the depth of caring that appeared when Nancy needed you: Julie Voelck of Ann Arbor, and Mary Ann Gholson of Davis. You saw Nancy as a whole person, and loved her well.

Thanks to Nancy's team from Yolo Hospice, the Threshold Choir, and her kind and gifted caregiver, Asenaca Hussein. For care over many years, thanks to Lisa Weber.

To Mary Benard and the staff at Skinner House, who said "Yes!" to this book, and have supported its creation throughout with passion and compassion, no thanks are large enough.

Nor are there thanks large enough to Nancy's parents, Lee and Marjorie Brooks. You gave her life, you instilled in her a love of words and a sense that her life was meant for service, and you were there for your sweet daughter at the end of her life.

Thanks beyond thanks to my friend, Nancy Morgan Shaffer. When I was installed in a previous ministry, I asked Nancy to give the charge to the minister. I was charged (I use passive voice here because she made it clear that it was not SHE who was charging me; she was simply finding words for the charge that was already there):

To find again and again
both the stillness and the community
that recall you to your being held in love,
so that you know indelibly:
there is nowhere you can go that God is not.

This is where it comes to rest. The living, loving, and giving of thanks, all endure. And still, there is light.

Mary McKinnon Ganz

Also by Nancy Shaffer

Instructions in Joy: Meditations

Skinner House Books, 2002

I would teach God with plates of pomegranates,
both before they were opened and after.
I would bring wet washcloths.
We would bury our faces and eat:
all that luminescent purple-red,
those clear-bright kernels fitted in tight rows
on small and tumbling hills—
and all that juice, so easily broken, sweet
and puckery at once. We would say nothing.
—*from* "Were I to Teach a Course on God"

"Nancy's world is riddled with epiphanies, her kitchen table an
altar set for communion, her anger pure, her sorrow sacramental.
Nancy reaches my soul. With unadorned honesty and eloquent
humility, she invites me first to bless the life I am given, and then
to redeem this gift by sharing it. She instructs my joy."
— Rev. Forrest Church, Unitarian Church of All Souls,
New York, New York

"Nancy Shaffer is a poet of extraordinary power."
— Rev. Tom Goldsmith, First Unitarian Church,
Salt Lake City, Utah